D1276719

ALSO BY BRUCE FEILER

ABRAHAM

A JOURNEY TO THE HEART OF THREE FAITHS

BRUCE FEILER

HarperLargePrint
An Imprint of HarperCollins*Publishers*

 For information address HarperCollins Publishers Inc., 10 East 53rd Street, New York, NY 10022.

HarperCollins books may be purchased for educational, business, or sales promotional use. For information please write: Special Markets Department, HarperCollins Publishers Inc., 10 East 53rd Street, New York, NY 10022.

FIRST HARPER LARGE PRINT EDITION

Library of Congress Cataloging-in-Publication Data

Feiler, Bruce S.
Abraham: a journey to the heart of three faiths / Bruce Feiler.—1st ed.
p. cm.
ISBN 0-380-97776-1 (hardcover)
1. Abraham (Biblical patriarch) I. Title.
BS580.A3 .F45 2002
222'.11092—dc21 2002070309
ISBN 0-06-051863-4
02 03 04 05 06 WBC/QW 10 9 8 7 6 5 4 3 2 1

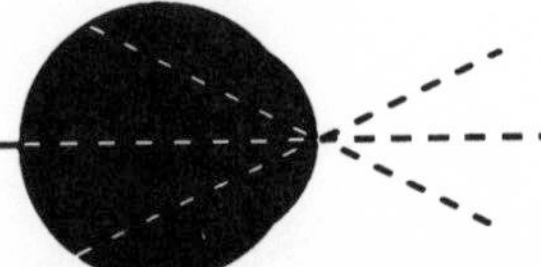

This Large Print Book carries the Seal of Approval of N.A.V.H.

For
Jessica Korn
and
Max Stier

Blessings

I will make your name great,
And you shall be a blessing.
I will bless those who bless you
And curse him that curses you;
And all the families of the earth
Shall bless themselves by you.

Genesis 12:2–3

CONTENTS

ROCK OF ABRAHAM

HOME

THEY START WALKING JUST AFTER DAWN. They stream through the streets, begin climbing the hills, and drop a few coins in the outstretched palms of the poor. They leave their houses, their lives, their neighbors, and come by themselves or in groups of two or three. Their heads are covered, their eyes downturned. They are alone. But when they pass through the gates and lift up their eyes, suddenly they are in an illuminated place, a familial place. They are home. No one is alone in Jerusalem: even the stones know your father.

Once inside, the stream divides. Christians turn north. Today is the last Friday before Christmas, and this afternoon monks will lead a somber procession carrying crosses down the Via Dolorosa. Jews turn south. Today is the last Friday of Hanukkah, and at sunset rabbis will hold a jubilant ceremony lighting six candles at the Western Wall. Muslims turn east. Today is the last Friday of Ramadan, and at noon clerics will hold a massive prayer service with two hundred thousand bending as one.

Today is not rare. Jerusalem is a touchstone of faith, and has been since before time began. The legends of monotheism are clear on one thing: Before there was time, there was water, and a darkness covered the deep. A piece of land emerged out of the water. That land is the Rock, and the rock is here. Adam was buried here. Solomon built here. Jesus prayed here. Muhammad ascended here.

And Abraham came here to sacrifice his son. Today that rock is a magnet of monotheism, an etched, worn mask of limestone, viewed by few alive today, touched by even fewer, hidden under a golden dome, and made more powerful by the incandescence that seems to surround it at every hour. The legends say God issued the first ray of light from the Rock. The ray pierced the darkness and filled his glorious land. The light in Jerusalem seems to fit that description perfectly. Washed by winter rains, as it is this morning, the air is the color of candlelight: pink, saffron, rose; turquoise, ruby, and bronze. It's a poignant irony that the light is all these colors, and yet the worshipers wear mostly white and black, as if they've yet to achieve the richness of the source.

Which is why they come in the first place. The Rock is considered the navel of the world, and the world, it often seems, wants to crawl through that breach and reenter the womb of the Lord. As my archaeologist friend and traveling companion Avner Goren says while we hurry through the streets and climb to a perch overlooking the city, "To live in Jerusalem is to feel more alive, more yourself. It's an honor, but it's a burden, too."

Stand here, you can see eternity. Stand here, you can touch the source.

Stand here, you can smell burning flesh.

At midmorning an explosion sucks life out of the air. I turn to Avner. "A bomb? A sonic boom?" "It's not a plane," he says. Gunfire riddles the air. A siren wails. The steady gait of worshipers becomes a parade of nervous glances. Every accessory is a provocation: a **talit,** a kaffiyeh, a **kippah,** a cross. Every stone is a potential threat. Men with machine guns hover, with walkie-talkie plugs in their ears, cigarettes dangling. Avner stops to hug an Arab shopkeeper.

"We are nervous today," Abdul says. "We are worried the Israeli police will provoke some young boy and fighting will erupt. Ramadan is always the worst."

Upstairs, on the balcony of a Jewish high school where we settle in to watch the day develop, a teenage Hasidic boy named Joshua, dressed in black, has come to observe the Muslim throng. "I appreciate the fact that they're religious," he says, "that they worship the same God as us. But that their prayers should put my life in danger—rocks and knives, killing policemen, fomenting blood and hate and murder. Just the other day I was walking in town when I heard an explosion. I turned and ran and there was another explosion. I started running in the other direction and then the car bomb went off. I was holding my stomach. I thought I was going to vomit. It was the first time I truly thought something was going to happen to me."

The legends say that wisdom and pain are the twin pillars of life. God pours these qualities into two symmetrical cones, then adjoins them at their tips, so that the abyss of pain meets the body of knowledge. The point where the two cones touch is the center of the cosmos. That point is the Rock, and it's where King David ached to build a Palace of Peace. But David made a mistake: He moved the Rock and in so doing unleashed the Waters of the Deep. "You cannot move me," the Rock announced. "I was put here to hold back the abyss."

"Since when?" David asked.

"Since God announced, 'I am the Lord thy God.' "

David inscribed God's name on the Rock and pushed it back into place. The deluge subsided. The touchstone is actually a capstone: remove it and death rushes forth.

By late morning a jittery calm prevails. Avner and I are overlooking the thirty-five-acre flagstone plaza of the Haram al-Sharif, or Temple Mount. On the southern tip is El-Aksa Mosque, the third holiest mosque in Islam. To the north is the Dome of the Rock, the splendid, cobalt blue octagon built over the Rock and topped with the twenty-four-karat dome that towers over Jerusalem's ecumenical skyline. Up above is the Mount of Olives and a cluster of churches marking Jesus' last steps. Down below are the sheer remains of the Second Temple perimeter, revered as the Western Wall. The defining spiritual fact of Jerusalem is this: Any panorama, any camera angle, any genuflection that encompasses one of these holy places will necessarily include at least one of the others.

But that doesn't prevent people from trying to blot out rival sites. On any day, one can meet worshipers with destruction in their hearts. Joshua, the devout Jewish boy who sits with us, munching on half-moon chocolate cookies, confesses to a fantasy. "We believe the messiah will come and rebuild the Third Temple and all the Jews will come. I look at the Mount, and all those Muslims, and try to envision that."

As a result of dreams like this, we are not alone on our perch. Four burly men in jeans and leather jackets have pushed us back from the rail and set up a table to survey the scene with Pinocchio-like binoculars and Uzis. A quick glance across the rooftops, sprouting television antennae and geraniums, reveals countless sentries like them. Every holy day is a possible holy war.

But the rhythm of prayer prevails. As noon approaches, hundreds of thousands have overflowed the Haram al-Sharif and lined the plaza under cypresses and palms. The muezzin makes the call, and just as he does the bells at Gethsemane Church begin to sound, ringing out a Christmas carol. No one seems to notice the clash, and maybe it's not a clash at all: Harmony, after all, is controlled dissonance. The imam, the chief cleric of El-Aksa, begins his sermon, and the leader of the security personnel translates the incendiaries. Today is Jerusalem Day, when mosques around the globe profess allegiance to this fractured city, **al-Quds,** the Holy.

Finally the climactic moment arrives. The sermon complete, the cavalcade of worshipers stand in single rows. The imam reads the opening lines of the Koran, and they bend, stand, kneel, touch their foreheads to the ground, touch again, then rise. The tidal effect is awesome, like waves in a sea of milk: more people assembled in one place to pray than occupy most hometowns. A brief pause ensues, then the second tide begins: bend, stand, kneel, touch the ground, then the recitation of the holiest words of all. **There is no God but God and Muhammad is the messenger of God.** Afterward the imam offers a blessing: **May God bless the prophet Muhammad and his people just like he blessed Abraham and his people.**

Then the city holds its breath.

I had been coming to Jerusalem often in recent years. My visits were part of a larger experience of trying to understand the roots of my identity by reentering the landscape of the Bible. I did most of my traveling during a rare bubble of peace, when going from one place to another was relatively easy. Now that bubble had burst, and the world that seemed joined together by the navel was suddenly unraveling around the very same hub: East and West; Arabs and Israelis; Jews, Christians, and Muslims. Words like **apocalypse, clash of civilizations, crusade, jihad** resounded in the headlines. "We are in a world war," Abdul, the Arab shopkeeper, had said, "a religious war, and it's based just outside my front door."

My experience in the region persuaded me that it's possible—maybe even necessary—to gain insight into a contemporary situation by turning away from the present and looking back to its historical source. Especially in matters of faith, even the most modern act is informed by centuries of intermingled belief, blood, and misunderstanding.

And in that conflagration, as it has for four millennia, one name echoes behind every conversation. One figure stands at the dawn of every subsequent endeavor. One individual holds the breadth of the past—and perhaps the dimensions of the future—in his life story.

Abraham.

The great patriarch of the Hebrew Bible is also the spiritual forefather of the New Testament and the grand holy architect of the Koran. Abraham is the shared ancestor of Judaism, Christianity, and Islam. He is the linchpin of the Arab-Israeli conflict. He is the centerpiece of the battle between the West and Islamic extremists. He is the father—in many cases, the purported **biological** father—of 12 million Jews, 2 billion Christians, and 1 billion Muslims around the world. He is history's first monotheist.

And he is largely unknown.

I wanted to know him. I wanted to understand his legacy—and his appeal. I wanted to discover how he managed to serve as the common origin for his myriad of descendants, even as they were busy shoving one another aside and claiming him as their own. I wanted to figure out whether he was a hopeless fount of war or a possible vessel for reconciliation.

But where could I find him? Abraham, if he existed at all, left no evidence—no buildings or rugs or love letters to his wife. Interviewing people who knew him was out of the question, obviously; yet half the people alive claim to be descended from him. The Hebrew Bible discusses his life, but so do the New Testament and the Koran—and they often disagree, even on basic matters. Going to places he visited, as fruitful as that has been for me and for others, also has its limitations, because Abraham's itinerary changed from generation to generation, and from religion to religion.

I would have to design an unconventional journey. If my previous experience in the region involved a journey through place—three continents, five countries, four war zones—this would be a journey through place **and** time—three religions, four millennia, one never-ending war. I would read, travel, seek out scholars, talk to religious leaders, visit his natural domain, even go home to mine, because I quickly realized that to understand Abraham I had to understand his heirs.

And there are billions of those. Despite countless revolutions in the history of ideas, Abraham remains a defining figure for half the world's believers. Muslims invoke him daily in their prayers, as do Jews. He appears repeatedly in the Christian liturgy. The most mesmerizing story of Abraham's life—his offering a son to God—plays a pivotal role in the holiest week of the Christian year, at Easter. The story is recited at the start of the holiest fortnight in Judaism, on Rosh Hashanah. The episode inspires the holiest day in Islam, **'Id al-Adha,** the Feast of the Sacrifice, at the climax of the Pilgrimage.

And yet the religions can't even agree on which son he tried to kill.

What they do concur in is that Abraham occupies such sacred space because he is the first person to understand that there is only **one** God. This is his greatest contribution to civilization and the shared endowment of the Abrahamic faiths. It gives him power but is also a flash point, as everyone wants dominion over that moment. Muhammad may be more important for Muslims, Jesus for Christians, and Moses for Jews; yet all three traditions go out of their way to link themselves to their common patriarch. It's as if Abraham were the Rock, tugging everyone to a common hearth, the highest place, the earliest place. The place closest to God. Control the Rock and you control Abraham. Control Abraham and you control the threshold to the divine.

And so I returned to Jerusalem. I came alone—as everyone does, in a sense—to an uncertain destination. I came because this is the best place to understand Abraham, and to understand what he revealed about God.

And because this is the best place to understand myself.

Dusk fell early in Jerusalem that Friday. The sun left a wake of lavender and ruby that clung to the clouds and gave them the appearance of mother-of-pearl. By four o'clock it was nearly dark.

I walked down to the plaza in front of the Wall, where revelers gathered for the lighting of the menorah. The day had passed with disquiet but no blood, leaving the city grateful but spent. The explosions, I realized, were as much a part of the landscape as olive trees and primeval tales. Tomorrow everyone would wake again and once more confront the ache of anxiety.

But now was a time for celebration. A man with a white beard, black coat, and circular fur hat stood on a platform just under the Dome. Before him was a ten-foot-long iron menorah, eight feet tall, with nine round oil caskets the size of paint buckets. He lit a torch and raised it into the air. The crowd began to chant: **Praised be thou, O Lord our God, king of the universe, who has wrought miracles for our forefathers, in days long ago, at this season.**

And then the moment **these** worshipers came for. The five hundred or so people gathered at the remains of the Second Temple, a place desecrated two thousand years earlier, then reclaimed by a small band of radical Jews, began to sing "Rock of Ages." It was the same song my mother made my family sing, atonally, awkwardly holding hands around hundreds of multicolored candles during countless nights in my childhood. And yet this time I couldn't sing; all I could do was listen—to the voices, the stones, that throbbing of fear I'd felt earlier in the day—as I heard the words anew. **And thy word broke their sword when our own strength failed us.**

And as I stood there, remembering, staring at the prayers folded into the Wall, I realized that in the diaspora of monotheism we think of these holidays as being radiant with joy, but here they are resplendent in pain as well. Ramadan is a story of fasting and replenishing, Christmas the story of exile and birth, Hanukkah the story of destruction and deliverance. The same holds for this place, the Rock, the place where life meets death. At the navel of the world, Muhammad left earth for heaven, then returned; Jesus left earth, then also returned. Abraham lay his son on the earth and offered to slaughter him.

Is that the model of holiness, the legacy of Abraham: to be prepared to kill for God?

After a few minutes, a man approached. He was short, with a cropped sandy beard and black **kippah** covering his head. David Willna had attended a Jewish day school in Los Angeles, then a Roman Catholic university. After winning fourteen thousand dollars on **Wheel of Fortune,** he decided to come to Israel for a year. Fifteen years later he hadn't left. I asked why, and he told me a story.

Two brothers live on either side of a hill. One is wealthy but has no family; the other has a large family but limited wealth. The rich brother decides one night that he is blessed with goods and, taking a sack of grain from his silo, carries it to the silo of his brother. The other brother decides that he is blessed with many children, and since his brother should at least have wealth, he takes a sack of grain from his silo and carries it to that of his brother. Each night they go through this process, and every morning each brother is astounded that he has the same amount of grain as the day before. Finally one night they meet at the top of the hill and realize what's been happening. They embrace and kiss each other.

And at that moment a heavenly voice declares, "This is the place where I can build my house on earth."

"That story is shared by all three religions," David said. "And our tradition says that this is that hill, long before the Temple, long before Abraham. And the point of the story is that this degree of brotherly love is necessary before God can be manifest in the world."

"So can God be manifest in the world?"

"You could not have written a script that would

say that today, after thousands of years, with all our technology and sophistication, we would still be fighting a war over this place, over the legacy of Abraham. But the reason is that this is the place of relationship. This is not only the spot where it is possible to connect with God, it's the spot where you can connect with God **only** if you understand what it means to connect with one another.

"The relationship between a person and another human being is what creates and allows for a relationship with God. If you're not capable of living with each other and getting along with each other, than you're not capable of having a relationship with God." He gestured up at the Wall, the Dome, the churches. They were illuminated in man-made light now, their brilliance a little too sharp.

Then he turned back to me. "So the question is not whether God can bring peace into the world. The question is: Can we?"

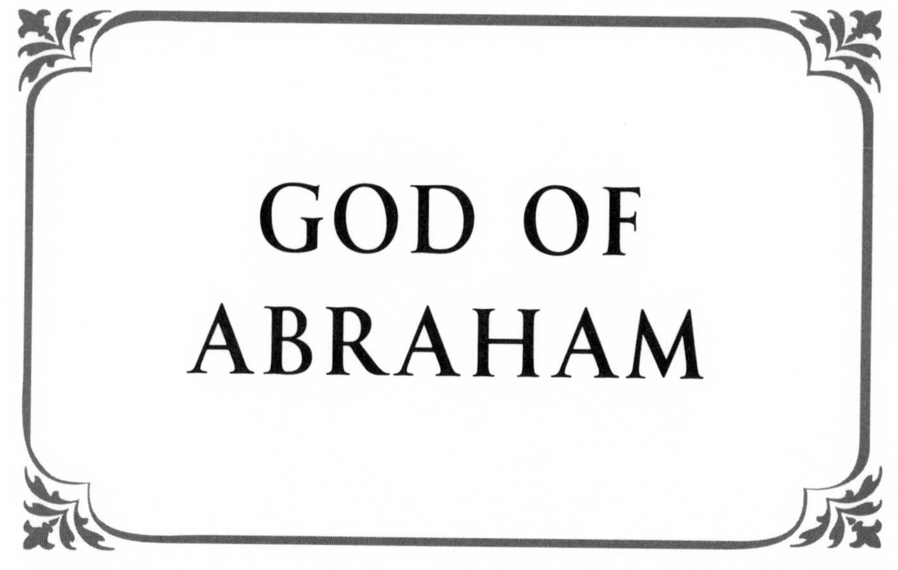

GOD OF ABRAHAM

1

BIRTH

HE IS OLD. HE OCCUPIES LITTLE SPACE. He hardly seems capable of riposte. Yet when he rouses a twinkle in his eye, he can still give life to the lifeless—and bring youth to the dead. He can also crush icons.

"So, Professor, what do we know about Abraham?" I ask.

"All we know about Abraham is in the Bible," he says. "In the ground, there's nothing."

Avraham Biran is sitting in his office overlooking the Old City, the same office he's occupied for thirty years, since he retired from his job as a diplomat and became the unofficial dean of biblical archaeologists. He wears a green pullover and a tobacco-stained grin. At ninety-three, he's near the age of the man he's spent his life pursuing when that man first appears in history, in Genesis 11.

"So does that mean he doesn't exist?" I first

came to see Professor Biran years earlier at the start of my biblical wanderings, and now I'm back at the beginning of another journey. I'm here to try to bring the dim early life of Abraham into some focus and to attempt to answer the question that gnaws at the core of my search: Was Abraham born at all? If so, when? And where?

"Oh, he exists," Professor Biran said. "Just look around you. But remember, archaeology cannot prove or disprove the Bible. I follow Albright, the founder of our field, in that the Bible as a book of divine inspiration needs no proof. At the same time, you can neither do archaeology in biblical lands nor study the Bible without being aware of the discoveries."

"So where do I look?"

"You look at the evidence, you look at the culture he came from, you look at the text."

"And what will I find?"

"Look, to me, these figures are real. I have no reason to doubt it. Whether all the details are correct, I don't know, and I don't really care. If you're looking for history, you'll be disappointed. If you're looking for Abraham, you won't be."

He has no mother. He has no past. He has no personality. The man who will redefine the world appears suddenly, almost as an afterthought, with no trumpet fanfare, no fluttering doves, in Genesis 11, verse 26: "When Terah had lived seventy years, he became the father of Abram, Nahor, and Haran." From this a-heroic start, Abram (the name in Hebrew means "the father is exalted" or "mighty father") goes on to abandon his father at age seventy-five, leave his homeland, move to Canaan, travel to Egypt, father two sons, change his name, cut off part of his penis, do the same for his teenager and newborn, exile his first son, attempt to kill his second, fight a world war, buy some land, bury his wife, father another family, and die at one hundred seventy-five.

Or did he? For most of the last four thousand years, the story of Abraham was almost universally believed—as the word of tradition, the word of scripture, the word of God, or all three. Beginning about two hundred years ago, many demanded proof. A wave of Jewish and Christian scholars scoured the Bible and concluded that the story had little basis in fact and, instead of being dictated by God, was cobbled together by competing scribes. "We attain no historical knowledge of the patriarchs," wrote Julius Wellhausen, the German scholar of the Bible and the Koran. Abraham, in particular, was "difficult to interpret."

Archaeologists responded to this affront by grabbing picks and heading for the hills. They dug in modern-day Iraq, where Genesis suggests Abraham was born. They excavated in southern Turkey, where he lived before departing to Canaan. They dug in Shechem, Bethel, and Beersheba, where he camped in the Promised Land. And while archaeologists didn't find a sign that said ABRAHAM SLEPT HERE, they found enough evidence connecting Abraham to the early second millennium B.C.E. that in 1949 William Albright declared: "There can be little doubt about the substantial historicity of the patriarchal narratives."

Such conviction was short-lived. A new generation of scholars rejected their elders' evidence as insufficient and their claims as romantic. Abraham was a product not of the time the story took place but of the time the Bible was written down, fifteen hundred years later, in the first millennium B.C.E. "The quest for the historical Abraham is basically a fruitless occupation," T. L. Thompson wrote in 1974. The story is little more than a collection of literary traditions, "best compared to other tales, like Hamlet or King Lear." From dust he had come, to dust he had returned.

But Abraham fought back. Tablets found in Nuzi, in northern Iraq, and elsewhere suggested that a variety of customs in the story, like having a child with a handmaid, were legal and well known at the time. Mass migrations from Mesopotamia to Canaan were noted around 1800 B.C.E. Slowly, a new consensus emerged that while precise evidence of Abraham is lacking, the story has countless examples suggesting deep oral roots that ground Abraham in his native soil.

These days, most scholars agree that Abraham—whether an actual figure or a composite—emerged from the world of Semitic tribes on the upper arm of the Fertile Crescent. Though the Bible, the most detailed account of his upbringing, does not mention Abraham's birthplace, the text says his brother Haran is born in Ur of the Chaldeans. Jewish and Christian scholars associate this place with Ur, the capital of ancient Sumer; Muslims associate it with Sanliurfa, in southern Turkey. The actual place is unknown.

Haran dies; Abraham and his surviving brother take wives; then Terah assembles the entire clan and decamps for Canaan. They arrive in the ancient crossroads of Harran, near Syria, where they settle. Far from random, this travel pattern is consistent with the lives of pastoral nomads, who traversed the region with herds, passed time near settled lands, then migrated to other places. Ancient documents describe an interactive society, in which wandering tribes were never far from urban areas, where they bought and sold goods. The Bible alludes to this lifestyle, calling Abraham a **Hebrew** and an **Aramean.** These and other variants, **Aramu** and **Arabu,** were common terms for "seminomad," until they were replaced with the catchall **Arab.**

But in telling the story of Abraham, the Bible is interested in much more than history. It takes elements of history, mixes them with elements of myth, and begins to mold them into a theme. Abraham is not a settled man, or a wandering man. He's a combination, who embodies in his upbringing a message he will come to represent: the perpetual stranger in a strange land, the outsider who longs to be the insider, the landless who longs for land, the pious who finds a palliative in God for his endlessly painful life.

The fact that Abraham is such a shadowy figure actually makes this point even more compelling. We must accept his story on faith rather than science. We must see him not as something we can prove but as something we must **believe,** just as we see God.

He's childless. He's aging. He's stuck in Harran. Abraham has lived nearly half of his life, and he's yet to do anything that arrests our attention. Why should we care?

If confronting the lack of history was the first step I needed to make to understand Abraham, considering his lack of childhood was the second. Most of the major characters in the historical line of the Bible are introduced as children, infants, or even prenatal predicaments. Large swaths of Genesis discuss Ishmael and Isaac before they're born. Jacob and Esau wrestle in their mother's womb. Joseph struggles as a teenager with the many-colored coat. The infant Moses is hidden in the bulrushes. The boy David fights Goliath. The newborn Jesus is wrapped in swaddling cloths.

Abraham is seventy-five years old before anything happens to him. The only thing we're told is that he comes from a long family line (the text traces his father back to Noah) and can't father children of his own. For Genesis, a narrative consumed with men, lineage, and power, the diminishing effect of this debility on Abraham is staggering. Our chief reaction upon meeting him is not admiration; it's indifference or pity. He's the ultimate blank slate: childless and childhoodless.

Since everything else in the Bible is purposeful, it seems safe to say that this lack of childhood must be purposeful, too. So what is the purpose?

God is looking for someone. He's searching for someone special. At the start of Genesis, in a state of agitated, fertile invention, God creates the world. He creates light and darkness; the earth and the seas; the sun and the moon; creatures of every kind. And after each one he declares his creation to be "good." Then he creates humankind, enjoins them to be fruitful and multiply, gives them dominion over other creatures, and, for the first time, declares his creation to be "very good." Humans are clearly central to God's world. He needs them. He wants them to be his representatives on earth.

But humans disappoint. Adam, in tasting the fruit, indicates that he prefers Eve to God, so God banishes them. Ten generations pass, during which God finds the earth to be corrupt and filled with violence. He is sorry he created humankind and decides to start over. This time he chooses Noah, a righteous man. But Noah, by getting drunk after sailing the ark, indicates that he prefers the bottle to God. Once again, God recedes. Ten more generations pass, during which God becomes outraged by humans' desire to unite and build a tower to the heavens. God does not want to be threatened. He wants to be imitated. He wants to be loved.

After so many failed experiments, God needs a new kind of human. He needs someone faithful, who won't disobey him and who will appreciate the blessings that he has to offer. Above all, God needs someone who needs **him** and who will rise to his lofty standards.

He needs Abraham.

Abraham inaugurates the twentieth generation of humans. Yet, from the beginning, he is different from the preceding ones: he is not righteous, he is not special. He's not godly in any way. Plus, he's restless. Along with his birth family and his wife, Sarai (like her husband, she will change her name later), he leaves one place for another but stops before he arrives and settles in a new place. He seems unsure. His life is suspended—and, worse, ruptured. He has no heir, no way to create the next ten generations, or even the **next** generation. As the text says, in its only biographical detail about these years, "Now Sarai was barren, she had no child."

The need for a son will dominate Abraham's life. Most heroic stories begin with a birth, a hopeful coming. The story of the father of Western civilization begins with the **absence** of birth, a listless despair. Abraham commands our attention by the sheer lack of command he exerts over his own life. In a story about creation, he cannot create. He is the anti-God.

Which may be the point.

In stories of heroic youth, the hero sets out to perform feats of bravery to win the hand of his beloved. The hero of a midlife quest has a different challenge. His is a darker, more inward-looking adventure that borders on madness as it reaches for the sublime. Think of Don Quixote, Oedipus. In midlife, a young man begins to grow old, to realize the inevitability of his death. As Jung observed, midlife is a tension between generativity, the feeling of being part of an ongoing process of creation, and stagnation, the sense of being stuck. Genesis is fundamentally the story of generativity. And Abraham, as he appears in chapter 11, risks disrupting that story. He has no life in him.

This crisis allows for the chief difference between Abraham and his ancestors: Unlike Adam and Noah, Abraham **needs** God. Specifically, Abraham needs the ability to create, and to get it he must turn to the Creator. Nelly Sachs, the German poet who won the Nobel Prize in 1966, viewed Abraham as a representative human, looking out at a decimated landscape, peering beyond the flames, aching for the divine.

> You have called me, Abram.
> And I long so much for you.

Abraham is not an individual man, or a historical man. He's the **ur** man, the man who reminds us that even though God may have cut the umbilical cord with humans, humans still need nourishment from God. This is precisely what makes Abraham so appealing to God. He's **not** God; he's human. The lesson of Abraham's early life is that being human is not being safe, or comfortable. Being human is being uncertain, being on the way to an unknown place. Being on the way to God. The emptiness of Abraham's invisible youth is the triumph of recognizing this necessity. His early years are a questioning, a yearning, a growing desperation, and finally a humble plea.

Help.

Late in my conversation with Avraham Biran, he told me a story. The first time he came to Jerusalem, as a young man, he visited many of the holy sites he had read about as a boy. His eyes twinkled brighter than ever. "And I felt nothing," he said. "The places themselves didn't touch me as much. What touched me was the stories."

And there are **hundreds** of stories.

The desperation at the heart of Abraham's early years—as appealing as it might make him to God—proved frustrating to his descendants and contributed to one of the more complex realities of Abraham's life: his unending evolution. Most historical figures leave behind a large body of knowledge—letters, journals, memories of associates—which gradually dissipates until people who invoke their names centuries later have only faint traces. Abraham is the opposite: The body of knowledge about his life **swells** over time, exponentially.

Probably less than 1 percent of the stories told about Abraham appear in the Bible. The vast majority did not even come into circulation until hundreds, even thousands of years after he would have lived. If you graphed all the stories about Abraham according to the date they entered the world, the resulting shape would look like a megaphone, with an invisible mouthpiece planted sometime in the second millennium B.C.E. that has expanded to a wide-open bell today.

For me this abundance presented a challenge. Looking for Abraham meant not just looking at the time he was born; it meant looking at any time anyone retold his story. Still, this was the only way to see Abraham. As a result, before I headed out onto the road and certainly before I sat down with any extremists, I had to venture in and out of various libraries. I had to turn pages covered in lore, legend, and sometimes hate. I had to begin to unravel the Abraham who had been constructed, from the ground up, by each tradition.

All three religions joined in this interpretive process, though Jews necessarily came first, probably beginning around the third century B.C.E. Every aspect of Abraham's life was open to retelling. First among these: his childhood. Denied a childhood in Genesis, he gets one in death; in fact, he gets more than one. In an elaborate, historical psychoanalysis, the children of Abraham slowly re-create the story of their forefather's early life in an effort to better understand their own. Abraham is like Jesus in this regard—the stories told about him **after** his death are as important as, if not more important than, the stories told about him **during** his life. This process initiates a rich paradox: God may have made humans in his image; we humans made Abraham in ours.

While the stories told about Abraham venture so far afield that they often appear made up, most interpreters were careful to anchor their tales in the text. With no clues about Abraham's boyhood, for example, interpreters turned to the Book of Joshua, in which God tells the Israelites, "Long ago your ancestors—Terah and his sons Abraham and Nahor—lived beyond the Euphrates and served other gods. Then I took your father Abraham from beyond the River and led him through all the land of Canaan."

"Aha!" the interpreters said. Abraham must have been different from his relatives because he **alone** was taken from beyond the Euphrates. He somehow **knew** that worshiping idols was wrong. From this simple hook, volumes were spun. In the Book of Jubilees, a noncanonical Jewish text from the second century B.C.E., the boy Abraham is presented as asking his father, a priest, what advantage idols serve, considering that they are mute. "I also know that, my son," Terah replies, "but what shall I do to the people who have ordered me to serve before them?"

In the Apocalypse of Abraham, from the first century C.E., the boy comes upon a stone god fallen over in his father's idol shop. When they lift the idol, it falls again, severing its head. No problem: the father promptly chisels a new body and attaches the old head to it. "What are these useless things that my father is doing?" Abraham muses. "Is he not rather a god to his gods? It would be more fitting for them to bow down to him."

While these stories show a brilliance of invention, their true gift lies in the way they appear to grow ineffably out of the text. Genesis suggests that Abraham's family lived in Ur of the Chaldeans. Archaeologists took this suggestion literally and went looking for Ur, but early interpreters took it etymologically and noted that **ur,** in Hebrew, means "fire" or "flame." Suddenly the line "I am the Lord who brought you out from [the fire] of the Chaldeans" took on new meaning.

Interpreters went to work. After Abraham confronts his father about the idols, Terah informs King Nimrod of Babylon, who orders the boy burnt in a furnace. A million people come to watch. Stripped to his underclothes and bound with linen, Abraham is cast into the furnace. For three days and nights he walks amid the fire, before finally emerging. "Why weren't you burnt?" Nimrod asks. "The God of heaven and earth delivered me," Abraham replies.

Ur was not the only word to inspire biographers. Chaldea, in lower Mesopotamia, was known in antiquity as the home of astronomy and astrology. For interpreters, this fact could mean only one thing: Abraham must have been an astronomer! As Jubilees reports, "Abram sat up during the night of the seventh month, so that he might observe the stars from evening until daybreak so that he might see what the nature of the year would be with respect to rain."

Other traditions have Abraham moving to Phoenicia to teach astronomy. Many have him teaching arithmetic and other sciences to Egyptians, who pass them on to the Greeks. Abraham, age seventy-five, a pastoral nomad, suddenly becomes the Albert Einstein of his day, going on the international lecture circuit, spreading knowledge, and earning the equivalents of Nobel Prizes in astronomy, mathematics, meteorology, as well as—just for his stamina—peace.

What's important about this process is that as early as a few hundred years after the Bible was written, Abraham begins to develop dimensions he doesn't have in the text. What's complicated about this process is that each writer tries to make Abraham speak to his generation, or to his particular target audience. One writer is a philosopher, so he wants to emphasize Abraham's reason. Another is a rabbi, so he wants to stress Abraham's piety. While these traditions may have made Abraham more appealing to their readers, they also risk making him less appealing to others. Astrology, for instance, is widely mocked today; saying Abraham was an astrologer actually **undermines** his credibility for our generation.

This situation leaves us in a challenging position—trying to glean more about Abraham while accepting that we're doing so through a prism that may tell us more about the author than the subject. I found this dilemma fascinating on one level but also daunting. Wait, you're telling me that if I want to understand Abraham I have to understand a different Abraham **every generation for four thousand years**? Even at a generous calculation of two generations every one hundred years, that's **eighty different Abrahams** I have to consider. How exhausting. How maddening.

How wishful. The real story is worse.

The eighty different Abrahams—stretched from antiquity to today—are only the ones created by **Jews.** Christians and Muslims have their own Abrahams. Eighty quickly becomes **two hundred and forty.** And Abraham quickly becomes unviewable. To put it in terms that a Chaldean could understand: Abraham is a Milky Way, not a North Star.

Again, I had no choice but to confront the thicket. It was off to another set of libraries and another assortment of scholars. In many ways, the geek in me—and eventually even the adventurer in me—found this process thrilling. It was like participating in a giant, three-dimensional scavenger hunt, where every clue in Judaism led to some desert hideaway in Christianity, led to some palm tree in Islam, under which was some spring—**yes!**—that suddenly cleared up some tangle described on the front page of that morning's newspaper.

The reason this pursuit proved so exciting is that to examine those hundreds of Abrahams—to understand how he evolved over time—is to understand what each religion values. And while many of those Abrahams would turn out to be incompatible with one another, **every one** agreed on one thing: Abraham believed in one God. And most agreed that he came to that view while still a boy. This biographical detail became so widely believed that it actually made it into scripture.

Christian interpreters, including ones gathered in the New Testament, like Paul and John, were interested less in Abraham's childhood than in subsequent events in his life. Islam, by contrast, was fascinated with Abraham's boyhood. The Koran was dictated to Muhammad ibn Abdullah, an Arab trader from the prestigious Qurysh tribe, over a period of twenty-two years, beginning in 610 C.E. The revelations came directly from Allah and were deeply painful for the prophet, who was caught unawares by his mission. "Never once did I receive a revelation," he said, "without thinking that my soul had been torn away from me." Muhammad believed not that he was founding a new religion but that he was restoring the primordial faith in one God. He also explained that he was bringing this true faith to Arabs, who, unlike their neighbors in the fertile regions of the Middle East, had yet to receive a prophet.

"I see Islam as a reformation in the context of monotheism," said Bill Graham, the chairman of the Department of Near Eastern Languages at Harvard and a leading historian of Islam. A trim, boyish man who arrived and departed from our meeting helmeted and on bicycle, Graham has an infectious North Carolina accent that makes every comment sound as avuncular and commanding as that of a grand southern judge. "The clear message is that Muhammad has come back with the Koran to revive and straighten the world, starting with the Arabs."

Because the Koran was simply reviving truths people already knew, its stories tend to evoke events rather than retell them in any sequential way. Stories about Abraham, for example, whom the Koran calls Ibrahim, are sprinkled throughout the text rather than grouped in the order Abraham may have lived them.

"The Koran is written in a referential style," Graham said. "It doesn't retell events, it refers to them. It uses the common rhetorical device 'Remember when . . . ,' as in 'Remember when Abraham did this. . . .' And you have to supply the **when.**" Because of the lack of a straight narrative, the experience of encountering the stories in the Koran is different from that of encountering them in Genesis. But the effect is the same: Abraham is less of a historical figure and more of a living person who makes points about human history.

"The Koran is more didactics than storytelling," Graham explained. "Everything is in service to the notion that we're all servants of God. Therefore, everything told about Abraham shows that in the midst of a pagan world he was an exemplar in his faith."

Even as a boy.

Abraham's childhood, ignored by the Bible, untouched by the New Testament, now makes its first appearance as scripture. And that childhood is remarkably similar to the legends that had been coalescing over the preceding millennium. In the sixth chapter, or sura, Abraham asks his father why he takes idols as gods. Outside, Abraham looks at the stars and concludes they are gods, until they disappear. The same follows for the moon and sun. Finally he realizes that one God must be behind them all. "I disown your idols. I will turn my face to him who has created the heavens and the earth, and will live a righteous life. I am no idolater."

The boy Abraham's next appearance is even more familiar. In one of the more famous Jewish legends, Abraham smashes the idols with a stick and attempts to blame the destruction on one of the idols. "Why are you mocking me?" his father asks. "Do these idols know anything?" The story in sura 21 is almost identical, with Abraham smashing the idols and blaming the destruction on the supreme idol. "Ask **them,** if they are able to speak," Abraham says. "You know they cannot speak," comes the reply.

The stunning similarity of these accounts presents two options. One, the story is true. Judaism, for one, holds that the oral tradition about Abraham and other figures was actually given by God on Mount Sinai along with the written text in the middle of the second millennium B.C.E. Islam also maintains that the Koran was dictated by God. The story of Abraham smashing the idols is therefore the word of God, and is sacrosanct. The other option is that the legends of Abraham were composed not by God but by God-intoxicated people. These legends then developed such currency in the Middle East that Muhammad picked them up from Jewish and Christian traders in Arabia. This situation would corroborate the scholarly view that Islam drew from existing elements in the region and made them accessible to a new and wider audience.

In either case, the significance of the shared heritage is clear: All three religions view Abraham's childhood in a powerfully similar way. At the root of Abraham's biography, there is harmony among all his descendants. The advantage of this universality cannot be underestimated. Abraham, across all religions and time, is devout, dedicated, capable of deductive reasoning, willing to struggle for his faith, and deft at using wit and logic to spread the divine message he alone understands. He is prophetic, heroic, charismatic. He is worthy of God.

The potential problem with this universality should also not be overlooked. One unintended lesson of Abraham's childhood is that individuals should feel free to liberate themselves from false religions, even in the face of resistance from their families, their nations, or their political leaders. This moral validates a tension that has existed until this day, with young people rejecting their parents' God in favor of their own. Abraham becomes a model not just for shared origins but also for fundamentalism, for the notion that **ye who hear God most clearly, hear most correctly.** Abraham, while still a boy, is denounced for his beliefs, even burned for his faith. Abraham, in other words, is not just the first monotheist. He's also the first martyr.

2

CALL

On a crisp Saturday morning in late October 1977, I stepped, never-shaven, to the pulpit of Mickve Israel Synagogue in Savannah, Georgia. I was dressed in a brand-new navy pin-striped suit, a white shirt, and a large-knotted tie with diagonal red, blue, and white stripes. My wavy blond hair was brushed twice over my ears. I was nervous.

As a clear light shined through the stained-glass windows, I carried a Torah from the open ark to the front of the small stage. I removed the silver pointer from the handles, then the crowns and breastplate, and finally the cloth mantle. Each gesture, done meticulously, took slightly longer than it should have. I unbuckled the clasp and unfurled the scroll on the podium. After reciting a brief prayer, I clasped the silver pointer in my palm, followed the direction of the rabbi, and began to recite in halting, uncertain Hebrew, **"Vayomer hashem el-Avram lech-lecha . . ."**

I was thirteen years old.

The words I was reading were the opening verses of Genesis 12, "The Lord said to Abram, 'Go forth . . .' "

In my family, a Bar Mitzvah was, to use the parlance of the boy I was at the time, a "big deal." I had started studying Hebrew years before. I practiced my portion at camp over the summer. Family and friends gathered from all over the country. The traditional coming-of-age ceremony for Jewish teenagers had even more meaning for me because the portion I was reading—in which God calls Abraham to leave his father's house and set off for the Promised Land—was the same one my brother had read at his Bar Mitzvah three years earlier. This story, which effectively begins the biological line of Abraham, also had resonance with my mother's family name, Abeshouse, or "House of Abraham."

I mentioned both of these connections in what was, for me, the most important part of the ceremony. After the prayers and the reading, the blessing and recitations, the rabbi sat down and I approached the podium alone to recite a short prayer of thanks I had composed. Silence filled the sanctuary as I stood by myself, before three hundred people, in a room my family had prayed in for nearly a century. The anticipation in the air, dense with sun and streaks of dust, the sheen of walnut pews and childhood memories, was palpable, but also warm and welcoming, the buttery embrace of tradition.

And suddenly I wasn't nervous. As I stood looking slightly over people's heads, the way my mother had taught me, reading from pages torn from a yellow legal pad, words written in green felt ink, my new suit suddenly didn't exist, my hair was no longer neatly trimmed, indeed my body effectively evaporated as I opened my mouth and became, in that instant, my voice.

If we can learn anything from the early life of Abraham it is this: God is listening when humans cry. He hears Abraham's plea in Harran, and responds with a call of his own. God's words in the beginning of Genesis 12 are among the most arresting in the Hebrew Bible, a transforming fracture in the history of humankind. All of Abraham's children, whatever their orientation, agree on one thing: God speaks not just to Abraham with these words, he speaks to every person who yearns.

But what exactly is he saying? This question has puzzled theologians, clerics, and Bar Mitzvah candidates for generations. The Call is a code, an encrypted blueprint for humanity. Decipher these words and we live with God's blessing; ignore them and we crumble like Babel.

The words themselves are simple and direct. "The Lord said to Abram, 'Go forth from your native land and from your father's house to the land that I will show you.

> I will make of you a great nation,
> And I will bless you;
> I will make your name great,
> And you shall be a blessing.
> I will bless those who bless you
> And curse him that curses you;
> And all the families of the earth
> Shall bless themselves by you.

With these words, God asserts his decision to create the world anew. As before, with Creation, he uses only words to call the world into existence, to conjure firm ground out of the chaos. Only this time, Abraham is the navel of the world, the sacred starting point. The Rock.

Despite their plainness, many things about these words stun: first, what they ask of Abraham; even more, what they promise in return. Covenants were well known in the Ancient Near East as formal contracts between two parties, usually involving mutual obligations sealed under oath. In the rigid forms such contracts followed, if duties were carried out, certain blessings ensued; if they were not, curses followed.

Though often referred to as a covenant, God's call to Abraham appears at first glance to include no tangible obligations on the part of the recipient. Unlike the covenant handed down at Mount Sinai, for example, this agreement comes with no commandments or laws that Abraham must follow in order to receive God's blessing. It would seem to be an expression of pure generosity on God's part, a one-way contract.

On closer inspection, Abraham is asked to do two things to fulfill his side of the contract. First, he must leave his native land and his father's house. This is an extraordinary request at any level, but it's made even more profound by the fact that he's aging, that his wife is barren, and that **he doesn't even know where he's going.** His destination is described merely as "the land that I will show you." Though later God will specifically promise Abraham that his descendants will be as numerous as the stars and that he will inherit all the land between the Euphrates and the Nile, at the moment God is being much more mysterious—and much more demanding.

This elusiveness leads to the second thing Abraham must do to fulfill the agreement: He must accept the legitimacy of the party offering the deal. This is no minor challenge and would seem much harder for Abraham than for, say, the Israelites at Mount Sinai. There, God has already sent the plagues, split the sea, rained down manna, and generally succored the former slaves in the desert. He then appears as thunder and lightning on the mountain itself, yet **still** the Israelites forge the golden calf and resist entering into a covenant with him.

Abraham, by contrast, witnesses no physical manifestation of God's existence—no burning bush, no dead frogs, no tablets, no water sprouting from a rock. Worse, the voice doesn't even introduce itself. Subsequent biblical figures learn that this disembodied eloquence belongs to the "God of Abraham" and usually hear a brief curriculum vitae. Abraham receives no such credentials.

So who does he think is making this promise? Later generations conclude that Abraham understood that the voice belonged to God, specifically the one and only God. All three religions are clear on this point. But the Bible, in fact, is not. If anything, it suggests otherwise. The voice that calls Abraham to Canaan belongs to **Yahweh,** often translated as "the Lord." Later, Abraham performs circumcision at the request of **El Shaddai,** or "Almighty God." He plants a tamarisk at the behest of **El Olam,** or "Everlasting God." Abraham, in other words, appears to serve several gods. Even **Yahweh** confirms this polymorphy, telling Moses that he appeared to Abraham as **El Shaddai.**

The suggestion in such passages is that Abraham, far from the complete monotheist of Moses, still retains echoes of the polytheism of his ancestors. He is a transitional figure, with a foot in both worlds. If anything, this position makes his trusting **Yahweh** even more remarkable. Abraham, rooted in a polytheistic society—a world where gods had form and physicality and were identified with tangible facets of daily life, like rocks and trees—is prepared to put his trust in an a-physical, indiscernible, **unprovable** god. Abraham is a visionary.

Which may be the most important point of all. However he understood the voice, the Call is still a monumental test for Abraham. With no knowledge of its supernatural source, no childhood spent studying its history, no attachment to it in any way, Abraham is forced to express superhuman devotion to this abstract request. Like the young man in the prototypical hero narrative, Abraham, in order to win the hand of his beloved, first has to declare his love, in deeds.

But what incentive! If God is asking the world from Abraham, he is offering the world back—and then some. God, who has already shown himself to be a butcher of genocidal fury, now reveals himself to be a suitor of formidable charms. He clearly wants Abraham to accept his proposal. Indeed, the breadth of his offer suggests he **needs** Abraham as much as Abraham needs him.

As a sign of his commitment, God promises Abraham that four things will happen to him: He will give birth to a great nation, he will be blessed, his name will be great, and his name will be a blessing to others. For good measure, God also vows to bless those who bless Abraham and curse those who curse him.

What's striking about this list is how it moves from the specific to the universal. It starts with what Abraham wants most: fertility. "I will make of you a great nation," God says. He promises, in effect, to give Abraham a son. The Creator—God—will make Abraham a creator, too, and, in so doing, transfer some of his glory to earth.

God's election of Abraham, as sacred as it is, also raises enormous risks. With Creation, God devised a world in which humans had dominion over other creatures but not over one another. Now he's introduced the notion of hierarchy. "I will bless those who bless you / And curse him that curses you." One group of humans receives God's blessing; another does not. There's still one God but now there are **two** groups of humans. Even before any tension arises **between** Abraham's offspring, a potentially bigger problem exists between all of his offspring and everyone else.

God seems to be aware of this possible fiasco, for having introduced it, he immediately attempts to ameliorate it. After promising to fulfill Abraham's individual need for biological fertility, God blows open the tent and offers Abraham the opportunity to provide surrogate, spiritual fertility to the entire world. It is in these words—"And all the families of the earth / Shall bless themselves by you"—that God elevates Abraham to the lofty status he will occupy for eternity.

Abraham is no longer just an individual, with individual needs. He has become God's proxy on earth. This symbolism is so profound that it reverberates down through the centuries, growing louder with each generation, until it echoes in billions of daily prayers to this day: Abraham was chosen not for his sake but for the sake of the world.

This is the ultimate power of the Call: It's a summons to the world to devote itself to God. God once again sends out an olive branch to humanity. If you put your life in my hands, he suggests, you will be rewarded. Since humans have flouted this branch in the past, God now requires a down payment: Do this today so you can get that tomorrow.

This demand for proof introduces a terrifying gap. In God's beckoning, the sacrifice is known, even the reward is known, but the route, the location, even the deliverer of the message are **unknown.** To be a descendant of Abraham is to live in that gap—to glance back at your native land, to peer ahead to your nameless destination, and to wonder, Do I have the courage to make the leap?

Abraham makes the leap and thus secures his reputation for all time. The text is so matter-of-fact it almost masks the significance: "Abram went forth as the Lord had commanded him." He does so silently, joining the covenant with his feet, not his words. The wandering man does what he does best, he walks. Only now he walks with God. And by doing so, Abraham leaves an indelible set of footprints: He doesn't **believe in** God; he **believes** God. He doesn't **ask for** proof; he **provides** the proof.

Abraham's unspoken covenant with God is so majestic it forms a central plank in all three Abrahamic faiths. Jews' relationship with the Call is the most complex. Did God initiate the relationship, interpreters wonder, or did Abraham? The latter books of the Hebrew Bible seem to place the glory with God. The Hebrew prophet Isaiah talks about God "redeeming" Abraham; the prophet Nehemiah praises God for "choosing" Abraham and bringing him forth out of Ur.

Traditionally, the Call is seen as initiating a process of migration that will culminate in Abraham being promised the land itself. As Nehemiah adds, "Finding his heart true to you, you made a covenant with him to give the land of the Canaanite, the Hittite, the Amorite," and others. "And you kept your word."

Later, when Jews were exiled from the Promised Land, Jewish interpreters began to emphasize that Abraham's going forth represented a more internal, spiritual journey. Abraham now becomes the suitor of God. Medieval rabbis, for example, said **lech-lecha** should be interpreted, "Go to yourself," as in go to your roots, find your true potential. As David Willna explained to me at the Wall: "As Jews we have to be committed to movement and growth, but it has to be for the right reasons. God doesn't need our help. We have to be doing it for ourselves."

Islam, meanwhile, stresses Abraham's submission to God and views the Call as a reward for his devotion. "Abraham was a paragon of piety," sura 16 says, "an upright man obedient to God." The word **muslim** actually means "one who submits to God," and the text says Abraham was of such exemplary morality that even as a boy in Babylon he was a **hanif,** one who practices pure monotheism.

The Koran suggests that it was in recognition of these traits that God chose Abraham and made him the leader of a great nation. As sura 2 says: "When the Lord put Abraham to the proof by enjoining on him certain commandments and Abraham fulfilled them, he said: 'I have appointed you a leader of mankind.'" The text calls this moment a **covenant,** and considers it the start of a nation of muslims that reaches fruition in Muhammad.

"Abraham is regarded as the founder of Islam as we understand it," said Sheikh Feisal Abdul Rauf, the imam of Masjid al-Farah Mosque in New York City and an international lecturer on Islam. A supremely serene man, Sheikh Abdul Rauf has receding white hair, a closely cropped beard, and a quiet but mesmerizing speaking style that deftly mixes an Oxonian English accent with the occasional Americanism for effect. He welcomed me into his Manhattan living room, covered with maroon-tinted bedouin rugs, and sat cross-legged and stocking-footed on a chair.

"I consider Abraham's covenant with God to be not so much a personal one," he continued. "It's the idea that Abraham will ensure that the belief in one God does not die with him. That he will pass this message along to his progeny and build a nation of people whose collective consciousness is defined by the surrender to God. Abraham's idea is the same as that of the U.S. Constitution, 'one nation under God.' "

Because Abraham surrendered so totally, God chose Abraham and set him on the straight path, taking him out of Babylon and delivering him into Syria, the geographic territory that includes Canaan. The Koran calls his destination the land "blessed for all mankind" and suggests Abraham agreed to go in order to worship God as he knew he must.

Like Judaism, Islam sees this as being as much of an inner journey as an outer one. "All spiritual-minded Muslims say that when we pray we should try to be in an Abrahamic state," said Sheikh Abdul Rauf. "We should take Abraham's viewpoint toward the world. We should try to be Abrahamic in our being."

And how would he describe being Abrahamic?

"First, complete devotion to God, even if it involves leaving your family and leaving your town. On another level, making our own contractual agreement with God. Each of us has a covenant to make with God, 'I will worship you as my God and you will take care of me.'

"And finally, knowing yourself on the deepest level. The prime objective of religion is to know God, but the only way to do that is to discover God within our own consciousness. This happened to Abraham, and it can happen to us. And anybody that happens to will choose to live a life in accordance with God's practice."

If Jews and Muslims consider the Call important, Christians view it as **the** defining act of Abraham's life. Before leaving for Jerusalem, I went to visit some old family friends in my hometown. The first person I went to see was John Lyons, who lived across the street from the house where I grew up. John, the oldest of nine Irish Catholic children, decided after lengthy deliberation to enter the priesthood. My mother was an important sounding board in his decision-making process, and a painting she made depicting his struggle hung on our dining room wall when I was a child.

"The Call of Abraham is critical for all God's children," Father John said. Approaching fifty with thinning red hair, he was dressed in a flannel shirt that made him look more like a lumberjack than like a priest. "Accepting that Call is what made him the Father of Faith."

I had come to talk about this notion of faith in Christianity, which I had read about but didn't quite understand. For many early Christians, faith was rooted in the story of Abraham's going forth. This connection was initially made by Paul, the first-century Jew who changed from being a persecutor of Christians to a missionary. For Paul, the primacy of Abraham was that his covenant with God was founded on faith, especially his "hoping against hope" in God's promise that he would have progeny despite his age. Abraham, Paul writes in Romans, "did not weaken in faith when he considered his own body, which was as good as dead."

Gentiles were capable of such faith, Paul stressed, and thus could be drawn into the arena of divine salvation. To be a child of Abraham is to respond to God's Call, to start a voyage, to become a stranger. As easy as it is to forget today—when Christianity is the dominant religion in half the world—early Christians felt a powerful sense of being alien. Departure is paramount to Christian identity.

"The lesson of Abraham," Father John explained, his voice plain and unornamented by years on the pulpit, "is you have to be willing to risk it all. You have to give up everything for God. Even in the New Testament, Jesus says unless you are willing to give up husband, wife, mother, father, and children, for the Kingdom of God, you are not worthy to follow me. The bottom line is if you're too comfortable, or too secure, or too into having **control,** then you won't be willing to trust God.

"And the Bible says, 'I want you to have total trust in me, Abraham.' You're not going to know where your next meal is coming from. You're not going to know where your next home is. If you're going to be in covenant with me, you have to trust me with every cell in your body. And if you do that, I will bless you.' "

As for Jews and Muslims, for Christians the Call involves an internal journey. As Father John said, "Most of us will never be called to take such a risk, but we have to be willing. We have to say, 'If you're calling me, God, I have to pray for the grace to accept.' You may not physically have to do it, but on the spiritual level you have to say to God, 'By following you I will find the peace of knowing that my life makes a difference.'

"It's like the Lord's Prayer. When I preach, I tell people this is a very scary prayer. Because when you pray that 'God's will be done,' you're saying, 'All right, God, I'm prepared to do your will.' Yet most of us want to do **our** will, because most of us are control freaks. We want the security of knowing that we have a house, we have a job, our children are protected, we've got a savings account. And God says that's not going to bring the security you really need in your life."

"But how do you know when God is really calling you?" I asked.

"It would be nice to get e-mails from God that say, 'I want you to be a rabbi, a writer, a priest.' I try to tell young people that if you want to understand what God is saying to you, you need to be quiet and focus on your life. The other day I drove my niece Mali into town. She's a sophomore in high school and didn't like the CDs I had in my car. I said, 'We can have silence.' She said, 'Oh, no, silence is boring!'

"Most of us are not comfortable with silence. We come into the house, we click on the stereo, we wake up to the TV, we fall asleep to the TV, we're always bombarded with music and words. Jesus, Abraham, they went out in the desert. They got away from all the distractions.

"I had a lady come to me recently and say, 'I need help deciding whether to have a heart transplant.' I said, 'I cannot give you any advice. The only thing I can tell you is you need to get away for a weekend, silence yourself, and pray. You should talk to people—your doctor, your husband. But in the final analysis, the only way you will find peace with your decision—the only way you'll find peace with God—is in silence."

"So the message of Abraham is to go away?"

"The message of Abraham is to be alone, to be quiet, and to listen. If you never hear the Call in the first place, you'll never know which way to go."

After leaving Father John, I stopped by Mickve Israel, the third oldest synagogue in the country and one of the defining places of my life. Arnie

Belzer was not the rabbi of my childhood, but in the years he's been in Savannah he's conducted my sister's wedding, eulogized my grandmother, and memorialized my uncle. He's an amiable, articulate man, with a penchant for nice cars and wing-fin silver sideburns. We sat in the sanctuary, as warm as I remember, and now with felt cushions in the pews. The Gothic arches were newly painted in almond. We opened to Genesis 12.

"What I see here, always, is Abraham answering this call from a God that's never been mentioned to him. And he doesn't question. **Show me something! Anything! What's your name?** Even Moses asks him that question. It's very powerful—an example of extraordinary trust. But it doesn't seem terribly Jewish. We put more emphasis on the Abraham who later argues with God. But what a great model for Islam, which admires acquiescence. And what a great model for Christianity, which puts primacy on faith."

"I'm wondering if it's a good model for life," I said. "Breaking away from his family brings him to his family."

"Until you break away, you're not grown up," Rabbi Belzer said, his New Jersey accent creeping through his adopted southern charm. "When I was in rabbinical school, a shrink told me that the minute you grow up is the minute it doesn't matter to you what your parents think. It was such a revelation to me. 'All right,' he said, 'you love your parents, you're always going to love your parents, but it's okay if they don't approve of what you're doing. It's okay if you leave your father's house and go someplace else. They might be disappointed. They might miss you a lot. But now you're grown up.'

"I know someone today who is fifty years old and hasn't gotten there yet. Fine. Abraham waited until late in his life to grow up and finally mature. But we all have to break away from our parents, even metaphorically. I don't want to tell this person, 'Soon, it won't matter, your parents are getting on.' But somehow he needs someone to say, '**lech-lecha.**' "

"So Abraham **is** a model."

" 'I will bless those who bless you, and curse him that curses you. And all the families of the earth shall bless themselves by you.' Clearly the blessing of monotheism is the blessing that's being talked about here. God says, 'Because of you, Abraham, the knowledge of me is going to the entire world.' I feel they were writing these words for me, for you, for anyone to look back and understand, 'I am part of this continuum. I'm still a blessing to the rest of the world.' "

I asked him if he thought Abraham's God was monotheistic, or perhaps something else.

"It doesn't matter. I always put together an invisible god and a monotheistic God. The significance of an invisible god is that it's not tied to a particular place; it's totally and completely portable. It allows you to go anyplace in the world. You're not leaving him. You'll always have him with you. We were building a completely portable religion."

"And that religion is?"

"Abrahamism. He's saying it's okay **not** to be in your native land, not to have land at all. He left his father's house, knowing his father would always be in his heart. I'll go someplace and try something new. I'll cast my lot with a portable god—the God of everyone, everywhere."

"So if what you're saying is true," I said, "then the Call is the most universal passage in the entire Abraham story."

"It is. The Call is saying that the relationship with God is not a relationship of belonging, it's a relationship of strangeness. We're all aliens. Abraham is blessed—the nations of the world are blessed—because he had the courage to go to another place and make himself a stranger. Because, believe me, at some time in our lives, all of us have to go to another place, too, and make **ourselves** strangers."

As he finished, my eyes began to roam around the room. They lit on the light above the ark, a shaft of pink from the stained glass, the line of plaques on the wall with the names of my family members who have died. My mom still likes to sit near that memorial.

I thought back to my Bar Mitzvah. Of all the events that weekend, one stands out in my mind. Saturday evening, after the ceremony, my parents invited about seventy friends and family to our house. I wore a brown corduroy suit, with a vest. About halfway through the party my father called me over to the bar that was set up near the kitchen. He ordered a gin and tonic. When it was ready, he put his arm around me, put the drink in my hand, and said, "Son, you're a man now. You're responsible for your own actions."

Sitting in the synagogue again, remembering that moment, thinking back on my childhood, I suddenly began to appreciate the grounding power of this room, the resonance of that Torah portion, the meaning of my father's words. Part of the inheritance of Abraham, I was discovering, was coming from a cozy place but also being prepared to **leave** that place. The only way to achieve your own family someday is first to depart the family you grew up with, which invariably brings you closer to the family you left behind. For me at least, the shock of separation helped me to appreciate the feeling of attachment that might otherwise have seemed smothering. The ache of being alone obliged me to discover the inheritance of home I carried around within me. And being apart from my parents allowed me to realize that being parented is a blessing—and that feeling independent is not incompatible with feeling protected.

Not until I reread the story of Abraham as an adult did I understand all the layers of mission in the narrative, or its purpose in my life. Fortunately, my parents had understood it first. I was a boy once in this place, and it was my dad himself who insisted, "Go forth."

CHILDREN OF ABRAHAM

3

ISHMAEL

THE DESERT IS GREEN THIS MORNING. The color startles the eye. A line of camels strolls by unawares. A hawk circles, unimpressed. But down in the rocky riverbed, caked from half a year in the sun but now starting to puddle, the verdure is comfort to a thirsty ground: Winter has come. Water is here.

"This is the desert of Beer-sheba," said Rami Harubi. "This is the desert of Abraham."

Rami Harubi is of that international breed, particularly common in the Middle East: someone prone to exclamations of natural poesy, literate in the language of sand, and often covered in dust. A desert person. Part eco-developer, part philosopher, and an old friend, Rami lives in the Negev and dreams of a paradise of perpetual wilderness. He is tall, graying, grand.

"You can see Abraham walking, just like those

bedouin," he said, pointing to a shepherd leading a huddle of sheep. "Today we are three weeks after the first rain. Smell it." He lifted a tuft of barely germinated grass, as short as a crew cut. It smelled like a picnic. "I have a special name for it, **virgin down.** From now, we start to feel the earth wake up. The earth is moist enough for the seeds to pop. It's wet enough for the ants to put their eggs into the ground. The bugs are waiting for this moment—and so are we. For the next six months we are happy."

Rami has brought me to the desert near Beersheba, where Abraham settles during much of his sojourn in the region, to show me what happens during a flash flood. He also wants to talk about the questions at the heart of Abraham's life: Will he have a son? Will he have more than one? If so, who will be his heir? The attempt to answer those questions will dominate Abraham's life for the rest of the Hebrew Bible, as well as the New Testament and the Koran. How these matters are resolved will lay the foundation for how Abraham's descendants will relate to one another for eternity.

"I usually bring my family to spend a night by this riverbed when it rains the first time," Rami said. "If you put your head on the ground, you can hear the water coming for about two kilometers." He made the sound of a hurricane. "It can roll stones and move cars, and if you're sleeping too deeply, you can find yourself in the Mediterranean—or not find yourself at all.

"But when the water comes, it just keeps going. All you want is to catch it, to hold it. **Wait, we need you!** And here comes the point." He walks me around the riverbed, where small puddles linger in limestone basins, and patches of pebbles show no water at all. Much of the ground splinters with the web of drought. "The animals drink the water in the puddles, so it never lasts. The real water is underneath the pebbles. If you want to survive here, you have to know the rules of the ground."

He places one hand flat in the air. "This is the desert." He places his other hand on top. "These are the people living here. Between the desert and the people there must be water. The story of Abraham is the story of water. He does two things here: He plants a tree and digs a well. That shows that he understood water, that he **became** water. He gave life to us all."

If finding water in the desert is difficult, then finding Abraham in the desert is even harder. His headwaters have disappeared, his tributaries overflow. But in the inundation of material about him, one truth is apparent. All three religions rely largely on the same root tradition and, in many cases, the same source text.

The prophets of the late Hebrew Bible refer to the Abraham of Genesis, the Gospels refer to the Abraham of Genesis, even the Koran refers to the Abraham of "the Book." Indeed, Genesis is the only place that explores the narrative of Abraham's life in any comprehensive way. The other books assume the reader already knows the basic story.

This assumption gives the biblical version a certain primacy in the story of Abraham but also raises a problem. The Bible is **not attempting to be comprehensive.** For every detail the story includes, even a casual reader craves the **dozen** details left out. "Wait!" the reader wants to cry. "Can I ask just a few questions before you move on?" The Bible would fail as history; it disappoints as reportage. But this may be exactly why it succeeds as narrative—and scripture.

The biblical story of Abraham is a triumph of literary ellipsis: the text gives us just enough details to deliver its myriad of messages, and not one syllable more. As a result, if I wanted to understand Abraham, even the Abraham that emerges in Christian and Islamic tradition, I quickly realized that I must begin with a careful reading of the story as it appears in Genesis.

And that story begins in earnest with the Call.

Once Abraham leaves Harran, the story shifts from the theoretical—"the land that I will show you"—to the practical—**where am I going?** The text reflects this change instantly. Abraham takes his wife, his nephew Lot, and all their possessions, and sets out "for the land of Canaan." In the next verse, they arrive in Shechem, in the Promised Land, and the Lord appears, saying, "I will give this land to your offspring." This is the second iteration of the promise, and the first that ties Abraham to a specific territory. This version also introduces a new dimension to the story: the geopolitical.

Abraham's ability to find himself in the center of world politics is not new; it began in antiquity. The entire scope of Ancient Near Eastern history played out on a narrow ribbon of water-fed land called the Fertile Crescent. The upper arm of the Fertile Crescent was Mesopotamia, the land between the Tigris and the Euphrates, which included the empires of Sumer, Babylon, and Assyria. The lower arm was Egypt and the Nile-basted civilization of the pharaohs. In between was the rain-dappled Mediterranean coast, more fragile land, with no great rivers to flood and, as a result, no great empires to terrorize their neighbors. If anything, the central strip of the Fertile Crescent—today's Lebanon, Syria, Israel, and the Palestinian Territories—was the strategic heart of the region, and both arms ached to control it. Neither did for terribly long, which only stoked the rivalry.

The story of Abraham as it appears in Genesis is a near-perfect personification of that battle. It's a story about the struggle for control of the Promised Land, a fertility battle in the cradle of fertility. Abraham is born in Mesopotamia. Bereft of land and seed, he travels to the Promised Land, where he immediately stakes claim to the territory. A drought strikes, and Abraham seeks refuge in Egypt.

The remainder of the story is an epic fight over Abraham's offspring, waged between two women, one from Mesopotamia, Sarah; the other from Egypt, Sarah's servant Hagar. Removed from enriched land, Abraham must summon the power to fertilize. To do this, he turns his life over to God. As Rami put it, "Abraham's innovation is to leave the land of rivers, to go someplace new, where he has to create a new world."

Arriving in Egypt, Abraham fears the pharaoh will kill him for Sarah, who is "beautiful to behold," so he asks his wife to say she's his sister. She does, and is promptly seduced by the pharaoh, who rewards Abraham with riches and cattle. God then rewards Sarah for her suffering by afflicting the pharaoh with plagues. The pharaoh responds by banishing the family.

Back in Canaan, Abraham's entourage is becoming so big that he and Lot must separate. Abraham gives Lot the nicer land, alongside Sodom and Gomorrah. When Lot is taken captive in a war pitting four kings against five, Abraham leads the coalition to rescue him. Our pitiful, impotent geriatric suddenly becomes a war hero!

And the world takes note. He begins to negotiate treaties with local leaders. The king of a Canaanite town, Melchizedek, blesses him and praises his Creator, "Blessed be Abram of God Most High, / Creator of heaven and earth." Abraham responds by giving Melchizedek a tenth of everything he has. One wants to cheer, rooting for Abraham's growth, the power he accumulates, his dignity. Abraham is not merely a man of faith, he's a man of strength and tolerance, too. He's not Machiavellian, Draconian, Napoleonic. He's Abrahamic—measured, moral, middle of the road.

But he's still not satisfied, and he takes out his frustration on God. When God appears after the military campaign and blithely reiterates his promise—"Your reward will be great"—Abraham talks back. "O Lord God, what can you give me, seeing that I shall die childless." He adds, forlornly, "Since you have granted me no offspring; my steward will be my heir." The silent one finally speaks, and his first words to God are words of desperation, even doubt.

God reacts immediately, dramatically escalating the promise he has been making for years. Your offspring shall be enslaved in a land not theirs, he tells Abraham. "But I will execute judgment on the nation they shall serve; and in the end they shall go free with great wealth." He adds, "To your offspring I give this land, from the river of Egypt to the great river, the river Euphrates."

At last Abraham has his prize—the most coveted land in the world is now his family's. And he earns this reward not in response to his prior silence but in answer to his newfound voice. By talking back to God, expressing his wavering faith, Abraham becomes even more human, and even more appealing. He has flesh, character; he's sympathetic. He strides atop the world, yet what he craves most is a son.

And so he begins to doubt. Abraham's wavering initiates a new phase in the story. Even before he fathers a great nation, Abraham fathers a great tradition, an interactive relationship with God, a struggle. Having given his down payment, Abraham now demands the same in return. Trust, but verify. Give me a son, he signals to God, or I can no longer trust you.

In my conversation with Rami, I asked him why he thought the story of Abraham was so concerned with children. "In the desert you have nothing," he said. "You are moving all the time. You have no house, no land. The only relationship you have is with your son, his son, and his son—a chain. You must connect with something, so you connect to your family."

Abraham has no family. The text reminds us bluntly at the start of Genesis 16: "Sarai, Abram's wife, had borne him no children." But now Sarah takes matters into her own hands. "Look," she tells Abraham, "the Lord has kept me from bearing. Consort with my maid; perhaps I shall have a son through her." Though legally Sarah's action is consistent with the ancient practice of surrogate motherhood, morally her act is troubling. The language suggests this. Sarah does not mention the maid's name, nor does she acknowledge that the resulting child might belong to the other woman. "Perhaps I shall have a son," she says.

Moreover, Sarah takes her maid and gives her to Abraham in an echo of the way Eve takes the fruit and gives it to Adam. Again the implication is unavoidable: Sarah is trying to wrest control of creation, which Abraham and God are already struggling over. Abraham may be wavering in his faith, but Sarah seems to have abandoned hers. Her act may be selfless, but it's also faithless.

Even more troubling is how passive Abraham becomes. The man who has just boldly stood up to God now meekly heeds Sarah's request—without speaking. The gallant war hero abroad is a wimp at home. "The thing that has always struck me about this story," said Carol Newsom, a professor at Emory's Candler School of Theology in Atlanta, "is that the moral sympathy of the story seems to be with Hagar and Ishmael, even though the author knows that our primary identification has to be with Abraham, Sarah, and Isaac." Newsom, a petite, fair-haired Alabaman with a Harvard Ph.D. is known as one of the leading interpreters of women in the Bible and a fiercely close reader of family relations in the text. "Yet the story constantly shows up their ignorance, flaws, and petty jealousies. It's astonishing. Rather than having simple identification, we're asked, in a sense, to identify doubly."

Sarah's gesture sets up a tension that will occupy history forever. Abraham's troubled paternity has now been compounded with even more deeply troubled maternity. "In literary narrative terms, you have two characters trying to occupy the same slot," said Newsom. "Sarah says, 'Let's move Hagar into my slot.' But you can't have such a writing over, a palimpsest. As soon as it doesn't work, you can see why."

Once Hagar becomes pregnant, Sarah grows jealous. Predictably, she lashes out at Abraham. "The wrong done me is your fault! I myself put my maid in your bosom; now that she sees that she is pregnant, I am lowered in her esteem." Abraham once again ducks responsibility. "Your maid is in your hands," he says. "Deal with her as you think right."

Sarah "afflicts" Hagar, the text says, using the same words later invoked to describe how the Israelites are treated by the pharaohs in Egypt, and Hagar responds the same way, by fleeing into the desert. The place Hagar goes—the wilderness of Shur—is the **exact same place** the Israelites go immediately after crossing the Red Sea. Again the Bible is sending a subtle message. All God's children are afflicted in some way. And when they are, God looks after them.

As if to confirm this point, the very next line has an angel of the Lord appearing to Hagar.

Only this time God sends her **back into the arms of affliction.** "Go back to your mistress, and submit to her harsh treatment." The protection given to Hagar stops far short of that given to the Israelites. Still, God clearly cares for her: the maidservant is the first person in Scripture to receive such a messenger, and God's messenger is the first to use her name. Indeed, God goes on to proclaim a blessing that rivals Abraham's in its scope and complexity.

The first thing he promises Hagar is innumerable children. "I will greatly increase your offspring." But God is specific with Hagar. She will bear a son and call him Ishmael, or "God hears." Ishmael, God says, shall be a "wild ass of a man; / his hand against everyone, / And everyone's hand against him."

Scholars dispute the meaning of these words, though most agree the term **wild ass,** instead of being a pejorative, refers to the character of the bedouin, specifically the wild desert ass that roams in herds. The subsequent line, "his hand against everyone," does suggest Ishmael's wilderness lifestyle will bring him into conflict with the world.

Still, the message here is nuanced. Hagar learns that her son will live in the desert (and not the watered land of Isaac), but she learns this **di-**

rectly from God. Hagar is the only woman to receive personally the divine blessing of descendants, making her, in effect, a female patriarch. As Carol Newsom put it, "Hagar, who earlier occupies the same place as Sarah, now occupies the same place as Abraham."

As if to celebrate her status, Hagar then speaks to God directly, "You are **El-roi,**" or "God of my vision." Hagar is the **only** person in the Bible—male or female—ever to call God by name. Sarah may still not be able to create anyone in her image, but Hagar creates God in hers.

All of the drama surrounding Sarah and Hagar obscures the important point: Abraham now has his heir! The exalted father is eighty-six when Ishmael is born, eleven years older than when he first heard God's promise. His great nation finally has its first citizen.

And make no mistake: first was definitely best in the Ancient Near East. According to the laws God dictated to Moses on Sinai, the firstborn son receives a double inheritance and succeeds his father as head of the family. This is true, Deuteronomy says, even if the mother of the first son is unloved. In Exodus, God goes even further: "The first issue of every womb among the Israelites is mine."

Given God's apparent preference for firstborns, why is it that Genesis seems to afford them such second-rate treatment? Cain murders his younger brother, Abel, and is cursed to be a fugitive wanderer. Esau, cheated of his birthright by his younger twin, Jacob, is banished to live outside the Promised Land. Jacob's firstborn, Reuben, commits incest, joins in selling Joseph into slavery, and is later toppled by his father. The fate of these firstborns is remarkably similar to the fate of Abraham's first issue, Ishmael, who is also exiled into the desert.

This consistency suggests an answer. For all its interest in rivers and the empires that emerge from them, the Bible distrusts such settled places. The text, in fact, seems ambivalent toward watered land in general. By contrast, the Bible is constantly sending people into the desert for redemption, because it's there, away from the ease of settled life, far removed from ready water, that they turn to God for sustenance.

The God of Genesis wants to be the water of life for his people. He wants his nation on earth to be protected but also to need him—to have the land but also to struggle. This desire requires complex maneuvering. Firstborns, the natural top dogs, achieve this balance by being plucked from their comfort and permanently dislocated. Secondborns, the natural underdogs, achieve this balance by inheriting the land but forever feeling alien. Both children, sons of man, thus become sons of God, living their lives in a state of perpetual agitation, comforted neither by their surroundings nor by their lineage, constantly longing for divine vindication.

But even such eternal craving is not enough for God. He wants human flesh as well. God appears thirteen years later and commands that Abraham circumcise the foreskin of his penis. Further, every male throughout the generations shall also be circumcised at the age of eight days. The struggle over fertility has now reached the level of flesh and blood. God demands a piece of human creation for himself; he leaves a sign of himself on every male. God thus becomes integral to every act of creation.

But he can't do it alone, so God asks Abraham to perform the first cuts. The Creator needs help from his human partner, who, now that he's a father, has proven that **he**'s a creator.

And Abraham does as he's asked—immediately. He circumcises himself at ninety-nine, Ishmael at thirteen, then **every male in his household,** including slaves. The significance of this order is often overlooked. Abraham is the first to receive the new compact, but Ishmael is the second. Isaac is not yet a gleam. Further, Abraham engraves this marker on everyone in his orbit, regardless of lineage. God's blessing is not limited to those among Abraham's descendants who will inherit the land; it goes to **anyone** associated with his household. Circumcision, later one of the most contentious features of Abraham's life, shows Abraham at his most inclusive.

As proof of this new expansive stature, it is circumcision that earns Abraham his new name. "And you shall no longer be called Abram," God announces, "but your name shall be Abraham, for I make you the father of a multitude of nations." (The word **Abraham** actually means "father of many nations.") Abram, the son of Terah, has now been re-created as the son of God. Now that he has God in his life (as well as on his body), he is ready to fulfill God's promise and become father of the world.

One puzzling aspect of Abraham's life is how little celebrated most of it is. Abraham has hardly been a towering figure in the history of art and entertainment. There is no Michelangelo statue that everyone can envision, as there is of David; no indelibly outstretched fingers on the ceiling of the Sistine Chapel, as there are for Adam. Joseph earned both a Thomas Mann trilogy and an Andrew Lloyd Webber musical (as well as a home video starring Donny Osmond).

Hollywood has been particularly neglectful of Abraham. Moses merits a Cecil B. DeMille epic and a DreamWorks animated blockbuster. Steven Spielberg and Harrison Ford spent an entire film looking for the lost ark of the covenant. And Jesus, well . . .

But no Abraham.

Yet Abraham's life would seem to fit the three-act model that Hollywood demands. Act one is his early life, climaxing in his call from God. Act two is his picaresque adventures on the road to Egypt and back, his growing frustration with God, the arrival of his son, and his dramatic sexual self-mutilation, which marks the culmination of his manhood but casts his potency in doubt. This sets up act three—the most action-packed of all—in which Abraham is trapped in a deadly love triangle, confronts a life-or-death decision with his first son, then must make a similar gruesome choice with his second.

The dilemma, for Hollywood, is that for all the action involving Abraham, his women, and their sons, the real story of Abraham is actually closer to an old-fashioned buddy picture involving him and God. Two figures with nothing in common get pushed together under extreme circumstances and are forced to figure out a way, against their natural instincts, to cooperate in order to save the world. What drama! What Oscar potential! But since one of these characters is invisible, filming this story becomes tricky.

In Genesis, the gentle back-and-forth between Abraham and his invisible interlocutor is precisely what gives the story its impact. And that struggle has just begun. After circumcision, the Lord appears to Abraham in the form of three men. Abraham immediately throws open his tent flaps, slaughters a calf, and asks Sarah to prepare a meal. As a reward, the men promise that Sarah shall soon have a son.

But she laughs. "I am withered, am I to have enjoyment—with my husband so old?" God is clearly miffed. "Is anything too wondrous for the Lord?" In response, Sarah actually lies to God—"I did not laugh"—but God has none of it. "You did laugh." Finally the men depart.

While Sarah has now been degraded by God, Abraham has been upgraded. As the Lord is leaving, he decides to tell Abraham a secret: He is considering destroying Sodom and Gomorrah for their sins. Abraham does something that would have been unthinkable a few years earlier: he begins to upbraid God. "Will you sweep away the innocent along with the guilty?" Abraham asks. "What if there should be fifty innocent within the city?" He ends in open outrage: "Far be it from you! Shall not the Judge of all the earth deal justly?"

Even more surprising, God begins to **negotiate** with him. If he finds fifty innocent people, God says, he won't do anything. What about forty-five? Abraham retorts. Okay, forty-five. And on they go in a dazzling downward spiral: forty, thirty, **twenty!** Until they finally agree on ten.

This reverse auction of human life is the most stunning passage of dialogue in the entire Abraham story, and possibly the whole Book of Genesis. Abraham, the warrior, has suddenly become the most daring and adept diplomat of antiquity: he in effect **creates** life that the Creator is about to destroy. Abraham, the once infertile man, is now nearly as fertile as God. The un-father now fathers people he doesn't even know, just because they might be moral. As a result, humans have a second protector on earth: If God forsakes them, humans can now turn to Abraham. Creation is no longer the sole dominion of rivers, or of God.

Abraham can create, too.

Sure enough, Abraham's newfound stature soon leads to more fertility. For a second time Abraham asks Sarah to lie and say she's his sister, this time to the king of Gerar. Once again God rewards her. "Sarah conceived and bore a son to Abraham in his old age." (The proximity of these two events has led some commentators to question Isaac's paternity.) Still, Abraham names the boy Isaac—"he laughs"—and circumcises him at eight days. But that's all the text cares to mention. Twenty-five years we have waited for this moment, and the Bible almost skips over it. Sarah is clearly happy. "God has brought me laughter," she says. But Abraham can't wait to take his son away from his mother, even throwing a feast on the day Isaac is weaned.

But Sarah is not to be elbowed out. If she's willing to stand up to God, she's certainly willing to do that—and more—to Abraham. One day she catches Ishmael and Isaac playing. Some interpreters have suggested that **playing** refers to sexual molestation since Ishmael is at least a teenager by now. But the word **metzachek** is a derivation of Isaac's name, **Yishaq,** which suggests boyish laughing.

Either way, Sarah acts swiftly and lethally. "Cast out that slave-woman and her son," she tells Abraham, "for the son of that slave shall not share in the inheritance with my son Isaac."

Abraham, however, does not share Sarah's preference for Isaac. Ishmael is still his firstborn. "The matter distressed Abraham greatly," the text says. But God comforts Abraham with a startling announcement. "Do not be distressed over the boy or your slave; whatever Sarah tells you, do as she says, for it is through Isaac that offspring shall be continued for you. As for the son of the slave-woman, I will make a nation of him, too, for he is your seed."

Once again, God sends a mixed message. On the one hand, he sides with the oppressor, and encourages Abraham to disinherit his firstborn son. God actually calls Isaac by name, and says that it's through him that Abraham's offspring shall be counted. The land, in other words, goes to the secondborn.

Ishmael, by contrast, goes unnamed, though God vows to make him a nation, the exact promise he initially made to Abraham. Isaac gets no equivalent grant. Also Ishmael carries Abraham's seed. The net effect of these intricacies is an uncomfortable but still purposeful balance: Isaac receives the land, but he does so in part through the malice of his mother. Ishmael goes into exile, but he does so with God's most exalted blessing and Abraham's deepest remorse.

In fact, Abraham does everything he can to resist sending his son to the desert. Unlike performing circumcision, which he does the "very day" God asks, this time Abraham stalls. The next morning he takes bread and a skin of water and gives them to Hagar, then he places them over her shoulder, then he does the same with the child.

Hagar leaves and wanders around the wilderness of Beer-sheba until she runs out of water, at which point she places Ishmael under a bush. The text plays their pain for maximum pathos. "Let me not look on as the child dies," Hagar wails. Then she bursts into tears.

And once again God hears. "Fear not," an angel cries to Hagar. "Lift up the boy and hold him by the hand." God then reveals a well of water. Ishmael has faced death directly, has done so at the hand of his father, but has been rescued at the last minute by God. This is his version of the Call: Cast out from his father's house, he survives only because of God's munificence. Created by Abraham, he is re-created by God. God refuses to give up the power of creation entirely.

This situation suggests an important lesson, one that will be echoed in the coming episode when Abraham nearly kills Isaac as well. Isaac and Ishmael, the driving force in the story of Abraham for a quarter of a century before they are born, become much less significant **after** they arrive. Having craved God's affection for decades when he **wasn't** a father, Abraham is unwilling to jeopardize that approval by choosing his sons over God.

Again, his behavior has lasting consequences. Abraham's children will spend the rest of their lives trying to claim the love of their father. Yet Abraham is too busy looking to God for affection to realize that his sons are looking for the same affection from him.

Perhaps the most striking feature of the story of Ishmael and Isaac is its balance: Neither son is a pure victor, or a pure loser. This literary masterstroke, however, has caused endless problems for their descendants.

Jewish interpreters were flummoxed by Ishmael. They agreed that, early in his life, Ishmael is deeply important to his father. When Abraham circumcises Ishmael and his household, for example, "he set up a hillock of foreskins, the sun shone upon them and they putrefied, and their odor ascended to the Lord like sweet incense." God announces, "When my children lapse into sinful ways, I will remember that odor in their favor and be filled with compassion for them."

But once Isaac is born, Jewish interpreters turn on Ishmael. Genesis says that after being rescued Ishmael marries an Egyptian and fathers twelve tribes. In the late first millennium B.C.E., these descendants came to be associated with bedouin tribes around the Middle East, first in the Negev, later in Arabia. Long before Christians or Muslims even considered this connection, Jewish writers identified Ishmael as the progenitor of the Arabs. Josephus, the Jewish historian from the first century C.E. who lived in Rome, wrote that the twelve tribes of Ishmael inhabited all the land from the Euphrates to the Red Sea. "They are an Arabian nation and name their tribes from these, both because of their own virtue and because of the dignity of Abraham their father."

Since these tribes were considered enemies of the Israelites, Jewish interpreters attributed all sorts of venal traits to them and, by extension, to their progenitor. As the commentary **Midrash Esther Rabbah** notes, "Of ten portions of stupidity in the world, nine were given to the Ishmaelites and one to the rest of the world. In the same manner, nine portions of robustness were allotted to the Ishmaelites and one to the rest of the world."

It was into this already malevolent interpretive tradition that Muhammad was born. While Jewish interpreters had linked Ishmael with the Arabs, Arab ones had not. Nothing about bedouins descending from Abraham appears in pre-Islamic Arabian sources. Early biographers of Muhammad, however, traced the lineage of the prophet's tribe back to Ishmael, through him to Abraham, and then back to Adam. Muhammad wanted to unite all Arabs under his tribe, the Qurysh, and to do so he needed to tie their heritage to a sacred source.

Ishmael was an important link in this chain, though he's hardly a major character in the Koran. Ishmael is mentioned only twelve times in the Koran's one hundred fourteen suras, and only one gives any indication of his character. Sura 19 says Ishmael was "a man of his word, an apostle, and a prophet. He enjoined prayer and almsgiving on his people, and his Lord was pleased with him."

Still, Muslim interpreters, in an effort to elevate Muhammad, set about elevating Ishmael. They began by resuscitating Hagar. Ibn Sa'd, a prominent scholar from the ninth century, said Hagar was the most trusted servant of the Tyrant, a shadowy figure corresponding to the pharaoh. Al-Kisa'i, a more inventive interpreter, says Hagar is actually the Tyrant's daughter. Either way, Hagar now has royal connections.

This imperial pedigree rubs off on Ishmael. Al-Kisa'i relates that as Abraham and Hagar finished the sexual act in which Ishmael was conceived, a heavenly voice proclaimed, "There is no god but God alone who has no partner." These are the same words, al-Kisa'i says, that Abraham uttered at the moment of his own birth.

The biggest contribution the Koran and its interpreters make to the life of Ishmael involves relocating him to Mecca. Instead of banishing Hagar and Ishmael to the Negev, Abraham actually **takes them** to Mecca, settles them there, then returns home. Left alone in the desert, Hagar runs seven times between two rocks looking for water before an angel appears and saves her. A vital shift is under way, moving the locus of the story away from the Fertile Crescent to Arabia, where Ishmael grows up to become a prominent Arab. Abraham even visits Ishmael in his new home. Sarah permits him to go, provided he doesn't dismount his steed.

On Abraham's first visit, Ishmael is out hunting, so Abraham talks with his wife, who is shrewish and inhospitable. She's also uncurious, not even asking his name. Abraham leaves a message for his son to "change the threshold of your house." Ishmael returns, smells his father, and interprets the message as disapproval of his wife. He immediately divorces and remarries.

Abraham returns, meets the new wife, and finds her charming and hospitable (though she also doesn't ask his name). She even goes so far as to wash and anoint his head with oil while he remains mounted. He leaves a message: "The threshold of your house is sound." Ishmael returns, smells his father, hears the message, and informs his wife, "My father approves of you."

On the surface, the Muslim traditions about Ishmael might seem to contradict the Jewish ones. But Jews have not seen it that way. In fact, in the centuries after Islam developed, many Muslim traditions began to appear in **Jewish** texts. In the eighth-century **Midrash Pirqe Rabbi Eliezer,** Ishmael takes a wife from the desert. Abraham visits his son, and the same routine transpires with the first and second wives, leading Ishmael to conclude that his father still loves him.

The similarity suggests that either this tradition originated in Jewish sources and traveled from there to Muslim ones or the other way around. Either way, the story's origin matters less than the towering fact that both traditions feel comfortable embracing it. While the details of Ishmael's life may differ slightly from one faith to another, from one generation to another, the essential message remains the same. Abraham expels Ishmael from the land, but he does not expel him from his sphere of love and paternity.

As is apparent beginning with the Call, the God of the Bible is interested in creating a great nation, on a specific piece of land, beginning with Abraham. Isaac is definitely the inheritor of that tradition. He is the **winner** of the struggle, so to speak, and Ishmael the displaced rival. As Carol Newsom said, "I think it would be disingenuous to say that this is anything other than a Jewish foundation story."

But given that clear literary function, the care and attention devoted to articulating Ishmael's future nobility become even **more** arresting. The Bible does not have a history of treating apostates or other ousted figures well. Adam and Eve are cursed. Abel is murdered. Lot's wife is turned into a pillar of salt. Ishmael, by contrast, is personally salvaged by God, fathers a dozen princes, and becomes the leader of a great nation. The crystalline moral here is that while God's land may go to one of Abraham's sons, God's blessing goes to both.

"Despite the story's interest in Abraham's heir," Carol Newsom said, "it still locates other relatives and indicates both the affection and the rivalry that exist among them. In that sense there's an honest description of social complexities. The story may not be **entirely** inclusivist, but it's close. Any attempt to claim Abraham uniquely runs afoul of the story."

Late in the morning I spent with Rami, I put a small rock in the middle of the riverbed. "This is Abraham," I said. Then I put two rocks underneath the first one in the shape of a family tree. "Here are Ishmael and Isaac. The question the world has been trying to answer for centuries is, Which direction does Abraham's lineage go?"

This is the kind of challenge that Rami loves. "If you are looking at the land," he said, "at buildings and stones, you might choose between this way and that." He then grabbed a handful of rocks and turned my family tree into concentric circles. "But if you're looking at the realm of ideas . . . it doesn't matter."

"And do you think stories have as much power as stones?"

"Much more. **Much** more. The story is the atmosphere of this place. It's around you all the time. You can move it. You can take it with you. You can do everything with it **except** carve it in stone."

He took his hand and swiped away his rocks, leaving only the rock of Abraham. "Abraham changed the world because he brought one idea to the world."

"So what's the idea?"

"The idea is that what's important is the power of ideas—**human** ideas. Not rivers. Not idols. Not stones. Not land. Abraham went into the desert, a place of nothing, and created something entirely new. And that something new was based on something invisible. He collected technology and know-how from all the places he visited. He mixed them with this big, unknowable, untouchable God, and he passed that down to both of his sons. And that's what changed the world. If we're fighting over stones, we're missing the point. Abraham was about a single idea, and that idea he gave to us all."

4

ISAAC

King David Street begins a few blocks from the Jaffa Gate in Jerusalem's Old City and extends south toward Bethlehem. The area, now home to luxurious hotels, banks, and a towering Armenian-style YMCA, was the first neighborhood settled outside the medieval walls.

About halfway down the street, a small Judaica shop sits at the end of a short plaza paved with Jerusalem stone. Inside, shelves lined with kiddush cups and Hanukkah menorahs mingle with dangling blue-and-white prayer shawls, and hundreds of knit, stitched, and gold-embroidered **kippot.** In the back of the store, a cardboard box about three feet wide spills onto the floor. A tangle of polished rams' horns claw out of the top like some snarl of petrified squid.

"Here's a good one," says the seventy-nine-year-old proprietor of B. Cohen & Sons. Dressed in black with gray curls tucked behind his ears, Binyomin Cohen is stooped, soft-spoken, with a wizardlike beard that drips down his chest and ends in a point. "The perfect shofar is about as long as two hands," he says. "This one is good because it curves to the right."

"The right?"

"Ever since they created the world there's been a big argument about right and left. Right is better because it's closer to God."

I have come to look at shofroth, the squiggling horns that were blown in the Bible at Mount Sinai and the Temple and that are now sounded annually on the Jewish New Year. The sound—raw, stuttering, bellowing—is made with the lips and lungs, for the horns have no amenities to improve their tonality. Jewish tradition suggests many reasons for blowing the shofar: The horn is reminiscent of God's revelation on Sinai, it reminds of the destruction of the Temple, it stirs the consciousness at the start of the days of penitence. But one reason resonates loudest. When I asked Mr. Cohen what he thought of when he heard the shofar, he answered, "The **akedah,**" the binding of Isaac.

"If you want to go to court," he said, "you take a good lawyer. The shofar is like a good lawyer. It reminds God of Abraham's obedience in being willing to sacrifice that which was more dear to him than life itself. As Rabbi Abbahu said, 'When you hear the shofar, recall the **akedah** and account it to your credit as if you bound yourself to the altar before me.' "

Though Binyomin Cohen has been selling shofroth for thirty years, he's been making them for twice that. When he was six, living by the Sea of Galilee, he and his friends were jealous of the men who blew the horns in synagogue. They went to the local butcher, procured a sheep's horn, and, following a practice unchanged for centuries, soaked it in hot water for several hours, then scraped out the interior. Left with a hollow, pointed shell, they heated a nail and hammered out a small mouthpiece. Then they polished the horn with pumice. The entire process took a month and a half. "We had to go to school during the day," he explained.

"And did it make a good sound?"

He raised his hands and shrugged his shoulders in the universal Yiddish expression for modest, sly, self-satisfaction: "**Hey, not for me to say. But if you really want to know the truth** . . ."

The binding of Abraham's favored son is the most celebrated episode in the patriarch's life. All three religions hail it as the ultimate expression of Abraham's relationship with God. But what the incident actually says, where it took place, even **which son is involved** are matters of centuries-old dispute. All of this makes the binding the most debated, the most misunderstood, and the most combustible event in the entire Abraham story.

In the opening words of Genesis 22, God once again suddenly and without preamble calls to his chosen one, "Abraham." This time, however, in a sign of Abraham's growing voice, the patriarch speaks back, "Here I am." "Take your son," God says, "your favored one, Isaac, whom you love, and go to the land of Moriah, and offer him there as a burnt offering on one of the heights which I will point out to you."

Once again God summons Abraham to go forth on a journey whose true purpose is not articulated and whose destination is not known. We have arrived at a second Call, a new **lech-lecha,** the final climax in Abraham's life with God. As exciting as it is to recognize the familiar chords of grand drama—sort of like hearing the reprise of a favored melody in a symphony—the text also sends a chilling message. **Four times** God has to identify which son Abraham should take—"your son, your favored one, Isaac, whom you love"—

as if Abraham isn't sure which son to take, which son is his favorite, or, once he knows it's Isaac, whether what he feels toward him is love. Even with Ishmael out of the picture, Isaac's status is still compromised.

Early the next morning, Abraham saddles his ass, takes Isaac and two servants, and sets out. On the third day, spotting the place from afar, he tells the servants, "The boy and I will go up there; we will worship and we will return to you." At the moment, Abraham, who says **we** will return, clearly believes Isaac will survive. But Isaac is not so sure. As they depart, he asks, "Father, here are the firestone and the wood; but where is the sheep for the burnt offering?" This is the most poignant moment in the story, and Abraham's response is matter-of-fact. "God will see to the sheep for his burnt offering, my son."

Abraham's treatment of his son—caring, but also cavalier and curt—reflects a larger ambivalence the Bible seems to feel for Isaac. Isaac is by far the least compelling of the patriarchs, and one of the least formidable major characters in the Pentateuch. Abraham is the father of the world, Jacob is the father of Israel, Isaac is merely the father of twins. The only memorable things about Isaac are what he **wasn't:** he wasn't unborn, he wasn't displaced, he wasn't sacrificed.

As for what he **was,** well, he was teased by his brother, he was coddled by his mother, he was nearly killed by his father, and, after Abraham's death, he was deceived by his wife and outwitted by **his** second son, Jacob. Isaac is not in the least bit godly. He's a simple man whom everyone takes advantage of.

At the outset of the binding, we don't know Isaac's age. Legions of artists have depicted him as a child, though the text suggests otherwise. Isaac himself carries the wood for the offering, which a young child couldn't do, and he's clearly capable of abstract reasoning, as shown by his question, "Where is the sheep?" Josephus said Isaac was twenty-five, while the Talmud proposes thirty-three, the same age as Jesus when he was crucified. One popular theory suggests he was older. Sarah was ninety when she had Isaac, and one hundred twenty-seven when she died. Because her death is depicted immediately following the binding and was triggered, many suggest, by news of the event, Isaac would have been thirty-seven.

However old Isaac is, he arrives at the spot with Abraham, who builds an altar. Abraham arranges the wood, binds his son, and lays Isaac on the altar atop the wood. Then he picks up the knife and prepares to slay his son. Will he? Will the great human hope, our surrogate creator, become as deadly a destroyer as God? And will Isaac just lie there quietly as his father slices his neck? We crave their inner thoughts. We await their debate with God.

No debate occurs. Isaac's silence at this moment may be unnerving, but Abraham's is unthinkable. The man who earlier berated God over the killing of people he didn't even know now seems willing to slay his own son. What was he thinking?

Interpreters have suggested possibilities. Perhaps Abraham knew Isaac was not going to die. That would explain his earlier comment that both would return. Perhaps Abraham believed Isaac really belonged to God, as suggested by the line from Exodus—"the first issue of every womb among the Israelites is mine." Finally, perhaps Abraham **trusted** God. He had faith. This would explain his line to Isaac, "God will provide."

But another possibility also arises. Almost all interpretations of the binding suggest it's a test, specifically a trial of Abraham's love for God: Would he be willing to do **whatever** God asked, however inhuman? Even the text takes this position, stating at the outset that "God put Abraham to the test." But God never tells Abraham it's a test. Even more, he **never asks Abraham to kill his son.** God demands only that Abraham take Isaac to a mountain and **offer** him as a burnt offering. Abraham is never explicitly given the order to slay his son. Early Jews, mindful of this nuance, referred to the event as an **offering,** not a **binding** and not a **sacrifice.** Death was not considered part of the story. As Binyomin Cohen said to me, quoting the Talmud, "A potter doesn't test defective jars, they would break. He only tests sound ones."

As a result, maybe Abraham is not being tested at all. Maybe he's **doing** the testing. Perhaps the episode is Abraham's way of testing God, specifically God's promise in the preceding chapter that Abraham's offspring will be continued through Isaac. Given that God pressured Abraham to expel Ishmael, Abraham surely would have been doubting God's loyalty. His attempt to kill Isaac thus becomes a way for Abraham to determine if God is a figure of mercy and compassion, which is deeply in question at the moment. If Isaac dies, then God is a liar. The offering, therefore, becomes Abraham's Call to God. Instead of "Go forth," Abraham says, "Come hither!"

And faced with **his** moment of decision, God acts. An angel of the Lord calls out, "Abraham!

Abraham!" And once again Abraham answers, "Here I am." "Do not raise your hand against the boy," the angel says, "or do anything to him. For now I know that you fear God, since you have not withheld your son, your favored one, from me."

Abraham looks up and spots a ram caught in a thicket by its horns. (This is the hook that links the shofar to the **akedah.**) Abraham offers the ram to God in lieu of his son. In return, the angel enhances God's pledge—"And your descendants shall seize the gates of their foes"—and Abraham returns alone to his servants. Whoever is doing the testing, Abraham emerges strengthened from the experience. No mention is made of Isaac.

The episode comes to a close.

But the consequences have just begun. The offering is Abraham's de facto answer to the Call and marks an inversion in the roles of Abraham and God. Instead of elevating Abraham to heaven, the incident brings God down to earth. Abraham has become the actor, God the reactor. Abraham thus inherits the mantle God has been dangling before him for a generation. He is God's partner. The human one has become unhuman; the ungodly one has become godlike.

Far from abstract, the difference is pronounced. Whereas in the beginning of the narrative Abraham **belonged** to God, now God, in a sense, **belongs** to Abraham. Forever after, God is referred to as the "God of Abraham." Their mutual trials completed, their love consummated, Abraham and God have now been irreparably fused. What fate has joined together, let no one put asunder.

Yet, of course, people tried.

About sixty miles north of Jerusalem, the Jezreel Valley climbs from the Jordan River in the east to Megiddo in the west. To the north is the placid Sea of Galilee. These plush hills, bursting year-round with wildflowers, persimmons, grapes, and avocados, have cradled some of religion's most pivotal events, from Joshua's conquest to Jesus' mission. The soil is littered with stones that speak of these moments, including a tiny synagogue in the town of Beit Alpha that contains the earliest known depiction of Abraham offering his son.

Beit Alpha synagogue was built in the sixth century C.E. by a small community of Jews. Designed to hold about three hundred worshipers, the limestone building faces south toward Jerusalem, with an apse and nave similar to those of churches at the time. The entire prayer hall is speckled with mosaics—tan, ocher, orange, and crimson. The tessellations depict an ark, a zodiac, and, closest to the door, a ten-foot-wide tableau of Abraham, Isaac, the ram, and a small arm of God crying, in Hebrew, "Do not raise your hand."

"Already by this time," said my archaeologist friend Avner Goren, "the **akedah** is the ultimate example of man's devotion to God. That's why it's at the center of a synagogue."

This was not always the case. After its description in Genesis 22, the binding is mentioned **noplace else** in the Hebrew Bible. Not David, Solomon, or any of the prophets refers to the story, though they allude to many other events in the patriarchs' lives. When later books cite Abraham, they mention his departure from Ur, his receipt of the covenant, his promise of land. Perhaps they were perplexed by the event. Perhaps they wanted to distance themselves from an allusion to child sacrifice. We don't know.

After centuries of neglect, however, the story began to gain prominence near the end of the first millennium B.C.E., during a time when the Israelites faced persecution. The Bible says Abraham's descendants were led out of slavery, then conquered the Promised Land by around 1000 B.C.E. They occupied the land for half a millennium, before being conquered themselves and sent into exile in 586 B.C.E. While in exile, leaders of the vanquished nation developed a series of practices and prayers that became the core of Judaism.

Even when they regained the land fifty years later, the Israelites no longer lived all together. Jews now practiced their religion in Mesopotamia, Egypt, and Arabia. For these communities, surrounded by hostile non-Jews, Abraham's offering of Isaac became a powerful symbol of the suffering a pious individual must endure for faith. As Philo, the Jewish philosopher who lived in Egypt in the first century B.C.E., wrote, Abraham served his Creator "out of love, with his whole heart."

The clearest mark of the new importance placed on the offering is that Isaac now becomes a willing victim. In Josephus's epic, **The Antiquities of the Jews,** which retells the story of the patriarchs, Abraham delivers a calm and reasoned speech to his son before the episode explaining his action. Isaac is so pleased that he assures Abraham he was not worthy of being born at all and will "readily resign himself" to the pleasures of God and his father. He then rushes to the altar to die.

For Jews of this period, deeply influenced by

Greek philosophy, the binding symbolized the power of reason to triumph over raw emotion, even parental love. In one popular story, told in the apocryphal book 4 Maccabees, a mother and her seven sons refuse to eat pork or meat sacrificed to idols and are brutally tortured and killed. "Sympathy for her children did not sway the mother of the young men; she was of the same mind as Abraham." The martyred priest Eliezer goes further, crying on his deathbed that Jews should be like Isaac: willing to sacrifice **themselves** for God. "O children of Abraham, die nobly for your religion!" Suddenly the offering is not just a test; it's the standard of piety.

The binding of Isaac, ignored for centuries, had been transformed by the time of Jesus into a defining moment in the life of Abraham and a powerful allegory for suffering Jews that they must be willing to look death in the face and still hold fast to themselves, their faith, and their father. Sacrificial death, even for Judaism, has become a path to divine redemption.

Christians picked up this view of the binding and transformed it even further: into the centerpiece of an iconic link between Abraham and Jesus.

A short walk west from the Temple Mount in the Old City rises one of the more oddly constructed buildings in Jerusalem, a sprawling, oft-remodeled basilica with extra chapels, cupolas, clerestories, and domes affixed to every surface. The Holy Sepulcher is to a church what a Picasso is to a portrait—a cubist vision of fractured beauty. The seventeen-hundred-year-old shrine that marks the spot where Jesus was crucified, entombed, and resurrected is so sanctified that dominion over its quadrants is divided disproportionally among the Greek Orthodox, Roman Catholics, Copts, Armenians, and Syrians. And a Muslim holds the key to the front door.

The Golgotha, also known as Calvary or Rock of the Crucifixion, is itself the locus of a two-floor chapel, the bottom controlled by the Greek Orthodox, the top divided between the Greeks and Roman Catholics. The Catholic quarter is decorated with three large mosaics: in the middle Mary Magdalene; on the left, Jesus just removed from the cross; and on the right, Abraham about to sacrifice Isaac. The image of Jesus sprawled on the unction stone is nearly identical to the image of Isaac on the altar. Both men are nude except for a cloth around their waists; their expressions show pained acceptance. Behind Jesus is a bush with no leaves; behind Isaac is a bush with a ram.

"It's clear that the message here is that Mount Moriah and Calvary are the same," explained Jessica Harani, a professor of religion at Tel Aviv University. "Abraham loves God so much that he will sacrifice his son. God loves humanity so much that he will sacrifice **his** son. There's an equation here. And this is how it should be."

"But there's one big difference," I said. "Abraham doesn't sacrifice his son."

"Christian typology sees the Christ as the fulfillment of all typologies."

For all their differences in later years, Christianity and Judaism shared something profound in the early centuries of the first millennium C.E.: Both were persecuted by the Romans. In this context, both religions needed models not just of faith but of faith in the face of challenge. Both found inspiration in Abraham's willingness to murder his son—and in Isaac's willingness to **be** murdered.

The connection between the binding and the crucifixion was first made by Paul. He placed the Golgotha at the heart of the new religion and saw in it the culmination of history: In one case, Abraham acts for the merit of Israel; in the other, God acts for the sake of all humanity. In both instances, God spares the life of the victim. "By faith Abraham, when put to the test, offered up

Isaac," Paul wrote in Hebrews 11. "He who had received the promises was ready to offer up his only son." Abraham considered the fact that God is able to raise someone from the dead—"and figuratively speaking, he did receive him back."

Other Christians of the era elaborated on this link. John calls Jesus the "Lamb of God." Irenaeus exhorts Christians to bear the cross for their faith as Isaac bore the wood for his offering. Tertullian notes that the reason Isaac carries his own wood to his sacrifice was a mystery kept secret until Christ was asked to carry **his** wooden cross to his sacrifice.

Moreover, Isaac, like Jesus, was born outside the realm of nature to a childless mother. Both births were announced by angels. The Gospels even set the date of Jesus' crucifixion at Passover, the same season in which Jewish interpreters place the offering of Isaac.

The idea of prefigurement—the notion that something that occurs in the Hebrew Bible represents something that occurs in the New Testament **even before it happened in real life**—powerfully joins the two stories together and reveals anew how Judaism and Christianity emerged out of the same crucible. But prefigurement also introduces the suggestion of hierarchy, which would later hobble relations between Jews and Christians.

For Christians, from now on, stories in the Hebrew Bible are no longer separate and autonomous; they become mere foreshadowings for events in the New Testament, where they reach their spiritual fulfillment. In this view, Jesus does not evoke Isaac, he supersedes him. The twin mosaics alongside the Golgotha, for example, include one powerful difference: Isaac has no golden halo; Jesus does.

Jesus, this reminds, actually died.

Isaac did not.

Or did he?

The early rise of Christianity corresponded with a period of retrenchment for Judaism, which suffered another mortal blow with the destruction of the Second Temple in 70 C.E. Jews of the era, already feeling victimized by the Romans, now felt even more imperiled. Few traditions experienced the impact of this change more than the episode on Moriah. The Christian interpretation of the story had become so powerful that Jewish interpreters felt the need to respond. Specifically, Jews followed the Christian lead and began to focus more on Isaac. Isaac, like the Jews, was a victim. Isaac, like the Jews, suffered in silence.

In one mark of this transformation, the Jewish name for the event shifted during this period, from **offering**, a word that appears in the story, to **binding**, a word that does not. (The common English term for the event, **sacrifice** or **near sacrifice**, also reflects this Christian influence.) In addition, the **akedah** first enters Jewish liturgy during this period, around the third century. Forever after, Jews would read the story of the binding during their New Year celebrations.

The significance of this change is that, in the early years of Christianity, Abraham has already gone from a figure of common origin to one the religions are struggling to control. Both religions want to present themselves as natural heirs to his legacy: "We're more like Abraham than you!"

This battle would only worsen over time. By the time of the Crusades, Christian-Jewish enmity had become so severe that Jewish interpreters took the ultimate step in attempting to reclaim their heritage for themselves. In the eleventh century, marauding Christians initiated a rash of bloody persecutions of Jews. In Mainz, Worms, Cologne, and elsewhere, Jews were asked to relinquish their religion and convert. If they declined, they were tortured. Rather than apostatize, many Jews opted to kill themselves and their children. Jewish prayer books at the time actually contained prayers to be recited before killing children and committing suicide.

"There is none better to sacrifice our lives to than our God," wrote a chronicler of Mainz, where three hundred died, in 1096. "Let everyone who has a knife inspect it lest it be flawed. Let him come forth and cut our throats for the sanctification of Him who Alone lives Eternally; and finally let him cut his own throat." Women cut the necks of their children, rabbis their flocks, lovers their beloveds—"until there was one flood of blood."

And what did they cry as they were committing mass suicide? "Ask ye now and see, was there ever such a holocaust as this since the days of Adam? When were there ever a thousand and a hundred sacrifices in one day, each and every one of them like the **akedah** of Isaac son of Abraham?"

Faced with their own deaths, Jews turned back to Abraham, and in so doing altered the notion of suffering that had existed for centuries. In antiquity, the children of Israel suffered because they had disobeyed God's laws. This malfeasance explained their punishments in the desert under Moses or in Israel after they set up a kingdom.

By contrast, medieval Jews began to see suffering as a sign of God's favor rather than his fury. Exemplary individuals are often asked to suffer for their righteous behavior, the rabbis said. Hardship is an indication of worthiness, not sin, and only strengthens those who are faithful. For proof they turned to Isaac. But in order to sell this idea of Isaac as the ultimate victim, interpreters had to make his story more closely parallel to the times. To do this they introduced a radical idea: Isaac, they said, actually **was** a victim. Abraham did kill his son.

The idea that Isaac died on Moriah has deep roots in Jewish interpretation. As Shalom Spiegel showed in his 1950 study, **The Last Trial,** commentators once again grounded their view firmly in the text. They pointed to the fact that Isaac does not return with Abraham from the mountain, and that the word for the ram, **hr,** is actually a cognate of **hryt,** or "end of days," which suggests Abraham understood that his descendants would be ensnared in thickets until the end of time.

But the biggest hook is that, as Abraham was binding his son, the angel called out **twice** to stop him. The first time he said, "Do not raise your hand." The second time, "Because you have done this and have not withheld your son, your favored son, I will bestow my blessing upon you." Interpreters pounced. **Why call out twice if Abraham actually stopped the first time?** Also, why say Abraham **did not withhold his favored son**?

Only one reason suggested itself: Abraham actually killed his son the first time. As Rabbi Ephraim of Bonn wrote in an influential twelfth-century poem, Abraham made haste, pinned Isaac down with his knees, and slaughtered him.

> Down upon him fell the resurrecting dew,
> and he revived.
> The father seized him then to slaughter him
> once more.
> Scripture, bear witness! Well-grounded is the
> fact:
> And the Lord called Abraham, even a second
> time from heaven.

Abraham then saw the ram, the interpreters suggested, and killed **it** the second time.

So if Isaac was actually dead for a limited time, what happened to him? He clearly returns later, fathers Esau and Jacob, and dies in old age. Here the commentaries get even more complex, and show their deepest allegiance to Christianity. Isaac, the rabbis said, actually went away for **three days**, then returned. In some versions he went to heaven; in others he went to the Garden of Eden, or even to study Torah. (The significance of three days actually predates Judaism and Christianity and was well known among Mesopotamian pagans as the time the gods traveled to the netherworld, then returned.)

Yet even for Jewish interpreters, the point is not that Isaac died but that he was **resurrected**. God revived him as a reward for his righteousness so he could provide salvation for his descendants. The idea that Isaac was sacrificed and reborn became so widespread that Jews in the Middle Ages began to put ashes on their foreheads to remember their slain forefather. Every Jew who faced trial became another Isaac. "Recall to our credit the many **akedahs,**" Rabbi Ephraim concludes. "The saints, men and women, slain for thy sake."

The idea of Isaac's death and resurrection is so powerful that once it entered the tradition it never entirely disappeared. If anything, Isaac's agony may be more responsible for the story's enduring influence. Abraham's test is so extraordinary it makes him seem remote in many ways, while Isaac's plight is more immediate. Abraham has become so godlike, he is no longer human. He is no longer us.

Isaac **is** us—our willingness to trust our fathers, our constant pain, our everlasting desire to be rewarded for our righteousness. At any point in history when innocent people have suffered, poets have cited Isaac as a beacon of dignity and injustice. The English poet Wilfred Owen invoked

Isaac's death in a vivid denunciation of fathers sending their sons off to die in World War I. An angel beseeches Abraham not to kill the lad, and even points to a ram to sacrifice instead. "But the old man would not so, but slew his son—/And half the seed of Europe, one by one."

The sculptor George Segal employed Abraham and Isaac the same way to commemorate the Kent State killings. Bob Dylan wielded Abraham similarly to protest Vietnam in "Highway 61 Revisited." God says to Abraham, "Kill me a son." "Abe says, 'Man, you must be puttin' me on.'" God says, "No." Abraham says, "Where should the killing be done?" God says, "Out on Highway 61." (The number 61 is believed to refer to a highway in Dylan's home state of Minnesota.)

But the idea of Isaac as a metaphor for needless death reached its definitive expression in the Holocaust. One Yiddish lullaby at the time wailed:

> You, my child, you are a member
> Of a holy congregation,
> Tender branch of a wandering tree,
> While, like Isaac to the **akedah**,
> The ship carries us across the sea.
>
> Sleep, my child; it's early morning.
> Soon the waves will quiet down.

In the fog so deeply hidden
Lurks our people's abiding power.

As Elie Wiesel has written, "All the pogroms, the crusades, the persecutions, the slaughters, the catastrophes, the massacres by sword and the liquidations by fire—each time it was Abraham leading his son to the altar, to the holocaust all over again."

But as Wiesel also emphasizes: Martyrdom, for all its endurance in religious history, is not the theme of the Jews, or the theme of the binding. Survival is. Isaac, whatever happens to him on Moriah, ultimately lives—as do his descendants. Jewish survival, in fact, depends on his survival, and draws on it for inspiration. This reassurance begins with his seemingly inappropriate name, **Yishaq,** "He laughs." As the first survivor, Isaac teaches the survivors of future Jewish history that it is possible to suffer and doubt for a lifetime yet not to lose the art of laughter.

Isaac, Wiesel suggests, never forgets the terror that befalls him on Moriah. He looks forever into the face of his father, sees the outstretched knife at his throat, and hears the saving call of God. And he knows that the shadow of his own death is illuminated by the light of his own endurance. And he knows, most of all, that in the glare of such calamity, there is only one response. He laughs, Wiesel imagines: "Nevertheless."

If the possibility that Isaac dies in the binding jostled the meaning of the story forever, another idea challenged it even more. What if Isaac wasn't the son?

On the ninth day of the month of Dhu l-Hijja, up to 2 million white-robed worshipers gather in the valley of Mina, just outside of Mecca. Under scorching sun, the worshipers prepare for the climactic events of the **Hajj,** the annual pilgrimage that all able-bodied Muslims who can afford it are called to make at least once. At dawn, the pilgrims take handfuls of pea-size pebbles, mount long ramps, and toss their pebbles at three giant stone pillars. These fifty-foot columns, actually conical in shape, represent the devil, who three times tried to tempt Abraham to disobey God by refusing to sacrifice his son. Abraham did not succumb.

The following morning, the pilgrims assemble again in the open plain. An imam leads a communal prayer, then takes a sheep at least one year old and turns it on its left side, facing Mecca. He recites the holy words **Allahu akbar,** "God is great," then carefully slits the animal's throat—

windpipe and jugular—in a single stroke. Blood forms in a puddle. The **'Id al-Adha,** or Feast of the Sacrifice, is the concluding rite of the pilgrimage and commemorates Abraham's sacrifice of the ram in lieu of killing his son. In Saudi Arabia alone, half a million goats, sheep, rams, cows, and camels are killed; the bulk of the meat is distributed to the poor.

"Eat of their flesh," the Koran says of the slaughtered animals, "and feed the uncomplaining beggar and demanding supplicant." The purpose of the act is not to feed God but to feed the souls of humans. As sura 22 says, "Their flesh and blood does not reach God; it is your piety that reaches him."

But as specific as the Koran is about the details of the slaughter and the distribution of the meat, it is strikingly **unspecific** about the details of the event that inspired the feast. Stop a random pilgrim in Mina, do a simple search on the Internet, interview a deeply believing Muslim anywhere in the world and ask whom Abraham went to sacrifice that day, and the answer will invariably be the same. As **The Concise Encyclopedia of Islam** concludes, "It is usually accepted in Islam that the sacrifice was to be of Ishmael."

But the Koran is not so clear.

The story of Abraham's near sacrifice is known in Arabic as the **dhabih,** from the verb "to cut, rend, or slit," and refers to both the method of slaughter and the victim. The event is described in sura 37, following the story of Abraham being tossed into Nimrod's flames as a child. Abraham cries, "Lord, grant me a righteous son." And the Lord complies. "We gave him news of a gentle son." When the son reaches the age when he could work, Abraham says to him, "My son, I dreamt that I was sacrificing you. Tell me what you think." The son replies, "Father, do as you are bidden. God willing, you shall find me steadfast."

Abraham lays the boy prostrate on his face, but as he does the Lord calls out, "Abraham, you have fulfilled your vision." "This was indeed a bitter test," God concludes. "We ransomed his son with a noble sacrifice and bestowed on him the praise of later generations. 'Peace be on Abraham.' "

The story ends with a first reference to a named son, "We gave him Isaac, a saintly prophet, and blessed them both."

The similarities with the biblical story are striking: Abraham receives a call to offer his son; he goes so far as to initiate the act; God intervenes and saves the boy. The similarities with biblical interpretation—both Jewish and Christian—are also notable: The boy is old enough to work and talk, Abraham actually consults his son, and the boy shows himself to be a willing victim.

But important differences also appear. First,

the event takes place in a dream, making it unclear if it ever actually occurred. Second, there is no mention of location, wood, fire, or a knife. Finally, and most notably, in the dream the son is **not named.** Isaac's name appears only after the narrative ends.

The lack of detail in the Koranic story is, in itself, not surprising. The Koran often excludes facts it assumes listeners already know and concentrates instead on the spiritual lesson of the events. And the message of this story comes through vividly: Abraham is a true believer, who submits to God's will, however extreme, and is rewarded for his efforts. God wants all humans to sacrifice our profane desires—even parental love—to serve a higher calling.

As Sheikh Feisal Abdul Rauf said, "The sense I get from reading the Koran is that the fundamental issue is that both Abraham **and** his son surrendered themselves to the ultimate sacrifice. When God asks you to do something, how far are you willing to go? Would you sacrifice as much as they did?"

Yet despite the clear intent of the story **not** to name the boy, the Koran appeared in the volatile religious climate of the seventh century, in which Jews, Christians, and Muslims were already beginning to wrestle over the ownership of the family of Abraham. As a result, Islamic interpreters felt the need to disentangle the ambiguity. The debate began immediately. The bulk of early interpreters examined the text and concluded that the son must be Isaac. They cited the fact that the sacrifice occurs relatively early in the life of Abraham, before he traveled to Mecca with Ishmael. Also, every time God promises Abraham a son in the Koran, the son is named as Isaac. Therefore, when Abraham prayed for a son at the start of the story, he would have been praying for Isaac.

Early Islamic interpreters added details to make Isaac even more appealing. The writer al-Suddi says Isaac asked his father to tighten his bonds so he will not squirm, to move the knife quickly, and to pull back his clothes so no blood will soil them and grieve Sarah. Abraham kisses Isaac, then throws him on his forehead (an interesting Muslim addition, given that worshipers touch their foreheads to the ground). Finally God intervenes.

The Isaac camp dominated in the early centuries of Islam, but in time it was matched by advocates of Ishmael. For their hook, these interpreters relied on the fact that God would not have asked Abraham to sacrifice Isaac since God had already promised Abraham and Sarah in the Koran that Isaac would have a son. God, by definition, does not break promises. Also, one source of tension in the story arises from the idea that Abraham is being asked to sacrifice his son when he would seem to be too old to have another. This drama would apply only to the first son, who is Ishmael.

As Sheikh Abdul Rauf put it, "There is no dispute among Jews, Christians, and Muslims that the commandment was to his **only** son. And there's no dispute that Ishmael was the oldest son."

Supporters of Ishmael also stress another point, a geopolitical one. The **dhabih** occurred in Mina, they say, after Ishmael had moved to the desert, during one of Abraham's visits. Jewish and Christian interpreters, they say, don't want to acknowledge Abraham's clear affinity for Ishmael. One interpreter, Tha'labi, in the eleventh century, tells of a Jewish sage who reports to his Muslim friends that Jews also know the real sacrificial son. "But they do envy you," the sage said, "the congregation of Arabs, that your father was the one that God commanded to sacrifice."

Ibn Kathir, writing later, goes even further, accusing Jews of "dishonestly and slanderously" introducing Isaac into the story, even though the Bible says Abraham went to sacrifice his only son, his favored son. "They forced this understanding because Isaac is their father while Ishmael is the father of the Arabs." As the commentator al-Tabarsi summarized the argument, "The proof for those who say that it was Isaac is that the Christians and Jews agree about it. The answer to that is that their agreement is no proof and their view is not acceptable."

Until the tenth century, Muslims debated the identity of the son, much as Jews and Christians scuffled over whether Isaac actually died. As another commentator, al-Tabari, said of the competing arguments, "If either was completely sound, we would not bother with any other." But neither side prevailed. The scholar Reuven Firestone collated more than two hundred medieval Islamic commentaries and concluded that one hundred thirty named Isaac as the son, one hundred thirty-three named Ishmael.

Yet over time Ishmael **did** prevail in the Islamic world, and the idea that Abraham may have taken Isaac faded into history. Firestone concluded that this has more to do with the struggle among the religions than with the struggle between Abraham and God. By the eleventh century, Islam preferred to rely on its own authoritative sources, and "as the genealogical connection with Abraham, Ishmael, and the northern Arabs became more firmly established, the Isaac legend was deemed increasingly suspect until it was eventually rejected."

For Muslims, Ishmael was the favored son, so he was the one Abraham took to sacrifice. What had been subject to debate became a matter of doctrine. And just as Christians believed their version of the story superseded the Jewish one, Muslims believed their version trumped both the Jewish **and** the Christian ones. A story nominally about submission to God had become the story of triumph in the name of God. As a result, the true victim of Abraham's offering proved to be not his son, or even the ram.

It was accord among his descendants.

As I was preparing to leave B. Cohen & Sons, I asked Binyomin Cohen how many children he had. "Ten," he said. And grandchildren? "Over fifty." What about great-grandchildren? He began to count. "Nine, ten, I don't remember."

"So would you sacrifice one of your sons?" I asked.

To my surprise he didn't hesitate. "Each of us performs our own **akedah,**" he said. "There are many things we do for God. He hasn't given me the order yet. But if he does give me the order, I would do it."

For Binyomin Cohen, as for so many people today, the idea of the ultimate sacrifice for God is not alien, it's immediate. It's an expression of their selflessness, their godliness, their willingness not to be bound by the world around them. And this, I was realizing, was one of the more troubling legacies of Abraham's life. Indeed, it may have been the one that set me off on this journey to begin with.

Abraham, I was discovering, is not just a gentle man of peace. He's as much a model for fanaticism as he is for moderation. He nurtured in his very behavior—in his conviction to break from his father, in his willingness to terrorize **both** of his sons—the intimate connection between faith and violence. And then, by elevating such conduct to the standard of piety, he stirred in his descendants a similar desire to lash out, to view pain as an arm of belief, and to use brutality to advance their vision of a divine-centered world.

For all the differences in how Jews, Christians, and Muslims interpret the story of the offering, by far the deeper revelation, I came to believe, is how all three religions have chosen to place the narrative of a father preparing to kill his son at the heart of their self-understanding. This fact is so fundamental that it's easy to overlook. But it shouldn't be. All three monotheistic faiths force their adherents to confront the most unimaginable of human pains: losing a child. The binding, the crucifixion, and the **dhabih**—often viewed as distinguishing the monotheistic faiths—actually illustrate their shared origins.

In a measure of this dark commonality, all three religions share a legend surrounding the offering. Immediately after the boy is saved, he lies on the altar, clutching the knife, the emotion of the ordeal flooding from his body. God tells him he will grant him any prayer. "O God, I pray that you grant me this," the boys says. "When any person in any era meets you at the gates of Heaven—whether they believe in you or not—I ask that you allow them to enter Paradise."

Faced with the phantom of his own elimination, Abraham's son responds with a Call of his own. He asks God to bless those who bless God **and** bless those who curse him. The comprehensive blessing God granted to Abraham is now returned as an even greater request from Abraham's son. Violence, in other words, can turn to virtue in an instant.

The last thing I asked Binyomin Cohen before I left was what was his favorite object in his store.

"I like customers," he said.

"I guess the situation is pretty bad," I said.

"It's very not good," he said. "I don't say bad. You cannot say bad."

"Why can you not say bad?"

"**Never say bad,**" he said. "If you get up in the morning and can open your eyes, it's good." He told me the story of how God, in Genesis 32, repeats to Jacob a promise made to Abraham to make his offspring "too numerous to count." "And the word **good** is written twice," Binyomin Cohen said. "This means if you say something is good, it will get better. And if you say something is bad, oh, you'll see what bad is."

Under the circumstances, these seemed like words of unrivaled beauty. In the midst of a war zone, just minutes after showing me the passage in Genesis that said Ishmael would hold a sword against Isaac forever, and just seconds after saying he would kill his child for God, he felt compelled to tell me that I should continue to be grateful. "If we say good things about Abraham," he said, "maybe the good will get better."

This is a holy place, I thought, where bad can be good, death can be sacred, and where no pain is enough to abandon God.

No wonder the story of the binding is so central to Jews, Christians, and Muslims, I thought. It's the part of Abraham's life that cuts closest to our veins and poses the question we hope never to face: Would I kill for God?

For many of Abraham's descendants, of course, the answer throughout history has been yes.

PEOPLE OF ABRAHAM

5

JEWS

MY EARS START POPPING JUST OUTSIDE the city. I get a mild headache soon after that. Within minutes of heading east from Jerusalem, the road starts dropping precipitously, through a flicker of rapidly changing climates: first cold and rain near the city, then clouds and a brushing of green grass on the mountains, then muggy air and blue sky at cliff's edge, and finally the hellish terrarium at the bottom of the world.

The Dead Sea, known in antiquity as the Salt Sea, serves as the backdrop for a number of pivotal events in the Hebrew Bible, including Sodom and Gomorrah, Mount Nebo, and Jericho. At the end of the first millennium B.C.E., it also served as the setting for a transformative moment in the history of the Bible—as well as the history of Abraham.

About thirteen hundred feet below sea level, on a ridge overlooking the northwestern shore of the sea, the remains of a small ancient community lie uncovered in the sun. The warren of rooms, large enough for a few hundred to eat, study, and cleanse themselves, is connected to the limestone bluff by a long aqueduct used to ferry purifying water. The redwood-colored hills where the aqueduct begins are so crumbly that they're pocked with dozens of alcoves, grottoes, and caves.

In the spring of 1947, a bedouin boy name Mohamed Adh-Dhib lost a goat along this ridge and, while looking for it, stumbled onto the mouth of a cave. He threw a pebble into the darkness and, instead of hearing the hoped-for bleat, heard the tinkling of breaking pottery. He was too scared to enter but returned the next day with a friend. The two squeezed through the opening and discovered nearly a dozen clay pots, several feet high, and the remains of many more.

They lifted the lids and found dark, oblong lumps coated in black pitch. The smell was putrid. Taking the lumps outside, they removed the pitch and linen wrapping and uncovered leather manuscripts, inscribed in parallel columns and occasionally crumbled. The characters were not Arabic, so they figured the most valuable part of the find was the leather: **new sandals!** Back at home they promptly carved out new straps for their sandals, then carried the largest scroll to a shoemaker in Bethlehem, who quickly realized he had something more precious than foot fodder.

What he had was a manuscript of the Book of Isaiah, a thousand years older than any known copy. Quickly the word began to spread: There's gold in them thar hills!

And God, too.

The Dead Sea Scrolls, which eventually totaled eight hundred once all the caves were scoured, revolutionized understanding of the Bible and the volatile political and religious climate that gave birth to Scripture. Penned by an extreme Jewish sect called the Essenes, who fled to the hills in the late centuries of the first millennium B.C.E. to live in extreme ritual purity, the manuscripts reveal an isolated community deeply devoted to studying the text of the Bible—and to understanding how that text affected their daily lives. This is the essence of the Abrahamic religions—taking ancient texts and making them timely **and** timeless, a process that is more vividly apparent in this community than anyplace else.

"What Qumran showed us," said Hanan Eschel, one of the leading archaeologists of that era, "is that as late as the third century B.C.E. different texts of the Bible were still circulating. Scribes were still taking bits of oral legends and combining them into one narrative." Eschel is a gentle, upstanding man who is deeply religious—he wears a **kippah**—yet fiercely committed to the evidence. Black-haired and a bit loping, with gesticulating hands, he reminded me of my elementary school science teacher in his ability to make, say, battery science, deeply matter **now**.

"So what happened in the third century to change that?" I asked. We were standing in the remains of a two-thousand-year-old library. The second floor had collapsed, revealing long desks where the scrolls were copied, even holes for inkwells. I had come to Qumran to try to understand this moment—when the text of the Bible finally became sacrosanct and believers began to reinterpret the story—because it represents a junction in the history of monotheism. It's what allowed Abraham, for example, to go from being a shadowy ancient figure to one who's perpetually alive, to go from one Abraham to two hundred and forty.

"What happened was that people finally felt they got it right," Eschel said. "The Bible became something spiritual that no one was allowed to change."

"And then?"

"Well, if people wanted to understand the text—understand how it related to their lives—they had to rejuvenate it. They had to retell the stories. The art of reinterpretation is the great innovation of this era, but, as we know, it's also what created a lot of problems for us."

Considering that I set out in search of what I thought was one Abraham at the heart of all three faiths, I was amazed by how much time I spent trying to figure out when one religion's Abraham ended and another began: Did the Real Abraham begin with the birth of Moses or the death of Jesus? Did the True Abraham begin with the death of Muhammad or the fall of Constantinople? And what about the Rise of the Bourgeoisie, that standby from college? Trying to track so many different Abrahams was like trying to track elevators in a skyscraper: dozens were in operation at any one time, some were rising, others were falling, each one stopped only at certain floors, and every carful had only one goal: Get me to heaven as fast as possible.

Eventually I concluded that, for all its chaotics, the history of Abraham as a cultural figure over the last four thousand years actually revolves around a number of critical moments that helped guarantee his enduring importance. The defining hour in his life—real or imagined—will always be when God chooses Abraham, plucking him from utter obscurity and allowing him to redefine the world.

The second phase in his story begins in the late first millennium B.C.E., when Jews start forging a religion out of their desert yore. In a critical moment often overlooked, early Jews also **chose** Abraham, summoning him out of the ethers of their past and promoting him to the status of founding father. As strange as it might seem today, when Abraham is known to many as the Father of the Jews, this status was never guaranteed. It was a **choice**.

The same goes for subsequent phases. Early Christians also chose Abraham. Early Muslims chose Abraham, too. Neither had to do this. History is cluttered with spiritual visionaries who completely reject the belief systems of their forebears. Abraham himself was one of these, after all. His heirs, by contrast, elected to emphasize their past. At **every transitional moment** in the evolution of religion, each subsequent incarnation of monotheism chose to link itself back to the same man.

The question of why the religions did this—

then what each one did with Abraham once it claimed him—would dominate Abraham's story for the subsequent two thousand years. As a result, if the first step I needed to make to understand Abraham was a close reading of his story, the next step was a close reading of how each religion reinterpreted that story.

I began, naturally, with Judaism. Long before Christians and Muslims set about reinterpreting Abraham, early Jews were the first to perform reconstructive surgery on their purported father.

The main reason Jews in places like Qumran were able to choose Abraham as their founder is that for much of Israelite history the patriarch was lost to his descendants. As arresting as the stories of Abraham, Ishmael, and Isaac are today, they were almost assuredly **unknown** to the Israelites who wandered for forty years in the desert, then conquered the Promised Land around 1200 B.C.E. By the time David overtook Jerusalem in 1000 B.C.E. and became king of a united Israel, Abraham was probably familiar to only a few leaders through oral wisps passed down through the generations.

"Do I think that the historical David knew

about Abraham?" asked Jon Levenson, a professor of comparative religion at Harvard and a leading authority on the history of Judaism. "I don't know. But I wouldn't be surprised if he didn't."

Yet David didn't need Abraham, because God makes a fresh covenant with him. "I will make the nations your heritage," God informs the Israelite king, "and the ends of the earth your possession." All the Israelites had to do was build a Temple to house God on earth and perform ritual sacrifices there, and God would ensure their well-being. No weekly Torah readings were required, no laws of kosher were observed. Judaism, as we know it, did not yet exist.

And it worked! David's son Solomon built a grand Temple in Jerusalem and paraded the Israelites to their strongest point in history. The Kingdom of Israel quickly became an empire to rival the ones in Egypt and Mesopotamia. But Mesopotamia soon fought back, and by the sixth century B.C.E. the Israelite kingdom was wiped from the Fertile Crescent. The bulk of Israelites were plucked from their homeland and shipped off to refugee camps in Babylon. The nations of the world were not Israel's heritage; the ends of the earth were not its possession. A crisis was at hand: God appeared to have broken his covenant.

Enter the Bible. During the exile, the spiritual leaders of Israel started to redefine their identity. They threw out the failed covenant of David and began looking for a new constitution. For that, they turned to their oral past. One figure they hit on was Moses. God promised him the land, helped him liberate the people, and gave him the laws. On Sinai, Moses received six hundred thirteen laws that govern everything from upholding the Sabbath to celebrating Passover. These suddenly became vital to a people thrust into turmoil.

But Moses wasn't enough. The leaders of the young faith needed not just a constitution but also a deep-rooted national mythology. They needed someone close to God yet not so wedded to the land, someone who embodied the noble history of the Israelites but who also typified their trials.

They needed Abraham.

Abraham was central to this newfound bond with the past because he stood at the beginning of the Israelite people. Also, God made a covenant with Abraham that predated the land. Abraham helped people cope with the crisis of exile because he himself had been exiled.

But who knew about Abraham? Certainly not most Israelites, who had few opportunities to hear their oral history. So elite scribes began to write down the story in a comprehensive way, a process that ultimately resulted in the Torah, the first five books of the Bible. In the middle of the fifth century B.C.E., Ezra, an Israelite priest, returned to Jerusalem from exile carrying this new written history. Repatriated Israelites had been living for nearly a century in the capital, where they rebuilt the Temple and tried to resume their former glory. Their efforts came up short. The Second Temple paled in comparison to the first, and the population numbered a meager twenty thousand, down from a quarter of a million.

Ezra was devastated to discover that the fledgling community was not practicing the piety now being observed in Babylon. At a New Year's festival, he publicly read aloud from the Torah. The initial response was grief—**How come no one told us this?**—followed by a rallying and a commitment to study the text. Many consider this the beginning of Judaism: God's will was now embodied by a text. The People of the Book was born.

Over the next few hundred years, the Israelites set about codifying their Book, gathering and recording all the oral stories, and making them available to the population. The invention in the third century B.C.E. of parchment—cheap, processed animal skins used in place of papyrus—

helped. "The difference," said Hanan Eschel, "was a simple material that could be found anywhere and not this rare plant found only in Egypt." The impact of parchment on the Bible—as well as on the history of ideas in general—is as great as that of the printing press nearly eighteen hundred years later.

But once the text reached final form—what scholars call **fixity**—the real work began. Suddenly the Israelites had Scripture that described the lives of their ancestors thousands of years earlier, but what difference did that make? They still needed to make that text relevant to **their** lives. They needed to build a causeway to the past. To do that they needed midrash.

Midrash, from the biblical root meaning "to search, inquire, or interpret," was invented by Jews in places like Qumran, then picked up by Christians and Muslims. "Qumran is a window where we can look at the process," Eschel said. "The people who lived here start reading Genesis, for example, and they feel, 'Well, it's hard to accept that Abraham is telling Sarah to say she's his sister.' They're clearly uncomfortable with the lesson this sends, so they change it. They rewrite the story."

In Judaism, midrash takes two forms. The first, **halakah,** involves interpreting the text to legislate conduct, such as what time to light Sabbath candles or how to make matzoh. "Without oral law, biblical law is so skeletal," said Jon Levenson, a soft-spoken West Virginian whose writings about Abraham are among the most astute I read. "We have no idea how to do a wedding. We have no idea how to do a funeral." Oral law is considered as binding as written law, and the rabbis held that it was dictated to Moses on Mount Sinai along with the Torah. At Qumran, sect members spent two-thirds of every night studying law.

The second form of midrash, **hagadah,** involves reinterpreting the narrative parts of the Bible to draw life lessons. Just as Abraham welcomed the messengers of God on their way to Sodom and Gomorrah, for example, so all Jews should welcome visitors to their homes. "It's very hard to know how to live the Abrahamic life," said Levenson. "What would you do? Get up and walk to Canaan? Tie your son to an altar? So they begin to take a figure who functions at the level of legend and turn him into a model for how Joe Six-Pack can live his life."

In short, early interpreters began to create a series of new-and-improved Abrahams. These late-model Abrahams, revised and updated, with a fresh coat of paint and a new set of tires, had the virtue of being immediate. They were **relevant.** But they were also different in significant ways from the previous Abraham, the one memorialized in Genesis. For the rabbis, these disparities posed a challenge.

The cliffs above Qumran are hardly impressive. The limestone is soft and easily eroded. The face is sheer, having been cleft abruptly when the Syrian-African Rift was forged by an earthquake 200 million years ago. The only vegetation is an occasional tuft of sage. The annual rainfall of the Dead Sea is two inches a year, compared with twenty-two in Jerusalem, only thirteen miles to the west.

After a short walk, Hanan Eschel led me into Cave Four, where fifteen hundred fragments from more than five hundred scrolls were found. I tossed a stone into the narrow opening and instead of a clinking sound, a flock of pigeons and Tristram's grackles fluttered into the air. The cave was dark, and cramped, at ten feet deep much smaller than I expected, able to keep a few eight-year-old boys occupied for not more than a few hours I would think.

"So why did they bring the manuscripts here?" I asked.

"They knew that the Romans would destroy everything, and they wanted to save them."

"It worked, I guess."

"It worked!"

The tension that drove the Essenes to go into the desert in the first place—and then to hide their scrolls in caves—is the same pressure that continues to haunt many Jews today: How should I relate to the larger world, especially when it's hostile to my religion? As an earnest, post–Bar Mitzvah teenager growing up in the American South, I participated in endless conversations about whether I was an **American** Jew or a **Jewish** American. Like many, I constantly pondered the question, Which identity do I put first? Do I join the prevailing culture and emphasize my similarities? Do I stand apart from the dominant culture and stress my particularities?

This unresolvable tension, I later realized, has existed since the birth of Judaism. Born in exile, surrounded by hostile populations, Judaism has always had tense relations with others. How Jews have responded to this struggle has defined their identity throughout history. It has also defined how they viewed their founding father.

Alexander the Great conquered Palestine in 333 B.C.E. and introduced a period of colonization that would subvert the Jews for the rest of antiquity—first to the Greeks, ultimately to the Romans. As they would for centuries, some Jews wanted to assimilate with their occupiers; others wanted to remain apart. Both camps turned to Abraham as their model.

For elite Jews, eager to fit into Greek and Roman life, Abraham became a symbol that Jews were deep down **just like everyone else.** Josephus, for example, ignored circumcision (too Jewish!) and stressed that a non-Jew like Abraham was at the heart of history. Philo underscored Abraham's role as a purveyor of science to the entire Mediterranean. This was Abraham as Father of Everyone.

Yet by far the more dramatic trend of the times took Abraham in the opposite direction. For besieged Jews, Abraham became their exclusive father who was chosen by God to pass on his blessing to them alone. They looked to Abraham to explain their plight. Just as Abraham says in Genesis 23 that he is "a stranger and a sojourner," so his descendants were strangers and sojourners under imperial rule. If they were forced to live with a bunker mentality, Jews wanted Abraham in their bunker. Forget his role as a blessing to all nations; we need him to bless ours.

The rise of Christianity and the Roman sacking of the Second Temple in 70 C.E. only accelerated the process by which Jews became more isolated—and more possessive of their biblical forefathers. In the absence of land or central Temple, being Jewish meant visiting a synagogue, observing law, reading Torah, and studying midrash. In this environment, beginning in the centuries after Christ and continuing for the next millennium, Abraham became an important tool to boost the morale of beleaguered Jews and help them withstand the pressure to convert. He became a political figure fighting for the preservation of Israel. But since Israel didn't **exist** during Abraham's life, the rabbis had to make some adjustments. The first sleight of hand they performed was to remove him from the restrictive confines of history and make him a timeless figure, a sort of guardian angel for Jews.

Suddenly, the rabbis write in their commentaries, Abraham was the reason God created the world. "But for thee I had not created the orb of the sun," God says in one midrash. "But for thee I had not created the moon." He was the protector of the afterlife. "In the Hereafter Abraham will sit at the entrance to the Underworld, and permit no circumcised Israelite to descend therein." He even sits next to God in eternity. Rabbi Judan tells a midrash that in the time-to-come, God will seat the messiah on his right and Abraham on his left. "Why am I on the left?" Abraham asks. "Because I am on **your** right," God says. Binyomin Cohen would be thrilled:

Abraham has become so exalted that God now sits on **Abraham's** right!

But the rabbis didn't stop at making Abraham semidivine; they also made him the ideal human: they made him the first Jew. This is actually trickier than making him God's left-hand man. Since the model Jew was one who observed Mosaic law, Abraham must now observe Mosaic law. Doing so would appear problematic, however, because Moses arrives some seven hundred years after Abraham. But the rabbis found an intriguing hook. In Genesis 26, God says that Abraham obeyed "my commandments, my laws, and my teachings."

Bingo! The rabbis interpreted this line to mean that Abraham knew and obeyed the laws before anyone else. In fact, he **invented** the laws. In the rabbinic portrayal that emerged during this period, Abraham speaks Hebrew. He sits in a learned academy studying midrash. He prays, tithes, observes the laws of purity, travels to the site of the Temple, even teaches grace after meals. He is the first to institute morning prayer and the first to prescribe using prayer shawls.

Abraham, the aging wanderer from Mesopotamia, the noble warrior who struggles with Sarah and Hagar over his heir, who expresses his religiosity by building altars and nearly sacrificing his son, now becomes a synagogue rabbi, keeping kosher, wearing a **kippah,** reading the Torah, and, no doubt, giving sermons that put his congregants to sleep.

Nearly every aspect of Jewish life now finds its origin in Abraham. The rabbis even discovered a way to credit him with inventing Passover, a holiday that on its surface celebrates the liberation of Abraham's descendants from slavery. Not anymore. When God's messengers come to visit on their way to Sodom and Gomorrah, and Abraham rushes to meet them, he drips blood since he has been circumcised only three days earlier. As a reward, God allows his descendants to evoke his righteousness by placing blood on their doorposts during Passover.

By the Middle Ages, Abraham had become so powerful he was nearly a saint. He prices every cow that's sold, ensures that kosher wine is cheaper, and saves the ships at sea from storms. A precious stone suspended from his neck brings immediate cure to anyone who beholds it; after his death the stone was suspended from the sun. In fact, Abraham may not have died at all; worms did not destroy his body once it was placed in the ground.

If these traits sound familiar, they are. Abraham had become a savior, a celestial figure who embodies divinity on earth, represents humans in the afterlife, and contains, in the deeds of his life, the scripture of God's intention. The Jewish notion of Abraham had become remarkably similar to the Christian notion of Jesus, in which Christ is the logos, the word and the law. Indeed, the two notions developed during the same period and no doubt influenced each other.

For Jews, under assault by Christians (and now Muslims as well), Abraham had become the redeemer, a sort of historical messiah before the actual messiah arrives. To be sure, not all rabbis maintained that Abraham was the exclusive protector of Jews. Numerous midrashim claimed that, because Abraham was circumcised at ninety-nine, he was essentially a convert and continued to welcome non-Jews into God's realm.

But the dominant strand of Judaism by the Middle Ages held that Abraham was no longer the figure who expressed God's universal blessing to humankind. Now he was a figure who sent his blessing exclusively to the descendants of Isaac. Abraham had become the singular possession of the Jews. The descendants of Ishmael, meanwhile, were cast aside. The text had been outstripped; the commentaries now reigned.

As a reader, as a citizen—and especially as a Jew—I was shocked to read about this collective, willful appropriation of Abraham. What happened to the kind, avuncular Abraham I learned about in Bar Mitzvah class? What happened to the universal, judicious Abraham who passes his blessing on to Ishmael **and** Isaac and who is called by God to be a blessing to "all the families of the earth"? More important, what should I do with this new Super Abraham now that I had learned about him?

To answer that question I went to see Rabbi David Rosen, the former chief rabbi of Ireland, one of Jerusalem's most prominent citizens, and the director of interreligious relations for the American Jewish Committee. Rabbi Rosen is an urbane man with a neatly trimmed dark beard and mellifluous speaking style that's one part Cambridge don, one part UN negotiator, one part Voice of God. Had he been alive in the time of Abraham, he would have been sent to mediate between Sarah and Hagar.

As a religion, Judaism considers this process of reconfiguring the Bible healthy, he noted. "What the rabbis are trying to do is reinforce the antiquity of the moral code they inherited. They see a danger that somebody might come along in the Jewish community and say, 'Look, Abraham didn't keep kosher and God says he's okay. Maybe it's not such a bad thing if I don't do these things.' "

They utilize the text as an educational tool, Rabbi Rosen added, in an effort to say that Abraham had divine inspiration and did these things even **before** God told them to Moses. "Of course from a historical point of view it's quite ridiculous. But I don't look at it in a scientific way. I look at what they did and see they have an important moral message they want to convey."

But as healthy as this approach may be, it lays the foundation for many of the problems the religions would face in the future. "There are dangers in this process," Rabbi Rosen agreed. "The sages themselves in the Talmud say that the day on which the oral law was written down is like the day the golden calf was made. They participated in this process, yet they say it was a terrible thing. Why? They are saying that the moment you write down the oral law you're also doing something a little bit obscene. You're taking something that's dynamic—the Torah—and you're making it rigid. You're taking the text and using it as **pretext** for your own ideas."

An even greater problem is that the rabbis subtly undermined the validity of the text by giving their own commentaries equal weight. This circumstance created what Rabbi Rosen called "anarchy" because the rabbis validated the idea of reinterpretation. Once Jewish commentators open the door by decoupling Abraham from his surroundings and recasting him in their image, Christian commentators come storming through, followed closely by Muslim commentators. If Abraham can become the First Jew, he can just as easily become the First Christian and the First Muslim. Soon the religions would be at war over their supposedly common heritage.

And suddenly the carefully balanced message of the Abraham story—that God cares for all his children—a tradition that existed for hundreds of years before the religions **themselves** existed, was put in jeopardy by the inheritors of that tradition. Abraham was a valuable catch. Control him, you control access to God. As a result, he became an irresistible invitation for identity theft: **Steal me, I'm yours!** Jews have no one to blame for this process but themselves. They initiated it, and they ultimately would pay a stiff price for it.

"You're dealing with a human problem," Rabbi Rosen said. "All good things can be prostituted. The question is, What is your motive? Medieval Christians prostituted biblical texts for their own purposes. Later, Muslims did the same. Even some rabbis today are doing this to promote Jewish nationalism. Everybody wants Abraham to be their exclusive father."

But how many believers today—Jews, Christians, or Muslims—actually understand this process? Certainly the religions themselves don't want to advertise that their view of Abraham evolved over time, and often in reaction to external forces. For me, just learning about this struggle for Abraham's identity—of which I had little knowledge despite countless hours of religious education as a child, decades of mainstream practice, and years of adult study—was disturbing, and a bit revolting.

My immediate reaction was to tune out all the commentaries. If you're going to tell me that Abraham is your exclusive domain when the text is clearly sending a different message, then **I don't want to hear it.** I'll stamp my feet, put my hands over my ears, and stick to the text.

"Your dilemma is a fascinating one," Rabbi Rosen said, his voice revealing a mix of bemusement and curiosity. "It will be interesting to see how you resolve this."

To do that, I'll even ask a more grown-up question: Why not reject the rabbis and their hoodwinks? Why not disclaim what began at Qumran?

The sun was just dipping behind the cliffs by the time we reached the farthest spot from the settlement, near Cave Eleven. The orange and red in the rocks' striations had grown richer as the day passed, the loneliness of the setting more acute.

The presence of so many caves in the hills reminded me of a similar arrangement in the Sinai, where early Christian monks came to live in the wilderness near the place Moses received the Ten Commandments. "In many ways, what happened here resembled what would happen later in Christianity with hermits who went into the desert," Hanan Eschel explained. "These believers left everything behind—no family, no personal belongings—and came here to serve God."

We settled onto a rock overlooking the Dead Sea. For something so grand and historic, the Dead Sea is always remarkably quiet. Maybe salt silences, or at least absorbs, sound.

I mentioned my growing frustration with the entire process of midrash. What the interpreters did might be ingenious, I said to Eschel, but it also created enormous problems.

"They didn't think about this," he said. "They were sure that what they were doing was important. They were trying to learn from history, and they didn't worry about the implications."

"But we know the implications," I said, "and the feeling I get—and I don't mean to be childish about it—is anger. Their innocent process soon spins out of control."

"I don't think that you're right. I think this is what makes Scripture interesting. The only other way would be to abandon the Bible. The world changed, and if you wanted to stay connected to other generations you had to have some way to change the text. If you couldn't write commentaries, the text would just freeze and be unimportant."

"But where do I put my allegiance?" I asked. I mentioned the rule in American baseball where a tie goes to the runner. "If there's a disagreement between the text and the commentaries, what do I do? Do I go with the text, do I go with the interpreters? Or do I just do my own interpretation?"

"The first thing you do is to realize that these interpreters were brilliant," he said. "They heard the text in a very creative way. And when you try to get into their minds, and understand what bothered them, you get a better sense of the text. The most important thing I tell my students is never underestimate those people, because the minute you think, Well, I'm smarter, then you won't understand what they were doing. And they knew what they were doing.

"And what they were doing is just what we're doing today," he continued. "They're trying to learn about what happened in Jerusalem, say, or Paris by looking at a verse in Scripture. It's a very old tradition. People in Qumran were doing the same thing. They were reading the Bible as applying both to the time of Abraham **and** to their time."

I mentioned that Jewish tradition holds that **halakah,** the oral law, is obligatory, but that **hagadah,** the interpretations of the narratives, are not. Even the rabbis said that often the **hagadah** contradict reason. "You don't seem threatened by the contradiction," I said.

"Good interpretation doesn't contradict. It's very hard to take the text and make it say the opposite of what it says. If you said Abraham went from Shechem to Harran, instead of the other way around, as Genesis says, it would be very hard. Sometimes they did radical exegesis, but the usual way was to add something."

"So as a practical matter, what you're saying is that you can read these various interpretations, enjoy them, but in the end you have to find your own meaning in the story."

"Right. But it will be an eclectic work. Every once in a while you'll think, Wow! This was so brilliant it must be what the author of the Bible was thinking about. So you'll take that idea, you'll throw in an idea from over here, and ultimately emphasize the things you're interested in. You'll do what a long list of people before you have done, but you'll do it today, in a world after

September 11, and what happened then will affect how you read Genesis."

"So what is the message of Genesis after September 11?"

He looked out at the sea for a second. The sky was becoming as orange as the stones. He was a remarkably relaxed man. The climb, the conversation, my petulance had done little to alter his serene confidence.

"If you ask me, it's a question of modesty," he said. "Why do religious people act the way they act? It's because of a lack of modesty. It's what happened in Jerusalem with Christian cults planning to blow up the Temple Mount to make way for the messiah. It's what happened in Israel with the murder of Prime Minister Yitzhak Rabin after he made peace with the Palestinians. Some people read the text and suffer from a lack of modesty. They really believed they had all the answers. I know that I don't have all the answers. I am trying to understand the text and the commentaries, and I know that somebody else will have more insights than I will."

He continued, "I think the same thing has happened with Islam. The Koran says that the people who believe in Muhammad should rule the world, yet they found out that the world is not functioning the way it's written in Scripture. It can't be a mistake in theology, so it must be a mistake in history—and this mistake must be temporary. The minute you get this notion in your head, you're allowed to change it. You're allowed to act for God.

"What I'm trying to do, especially in this part of the world, is to teach people to be more modest. To explain to them that they don't have all the answers. If you'll be modest, you'll probably understand the text better, and there's much less chance that you'll do awful things in the name of God."

"So can you find a basis in the Abraham story for modesty?"

He smiled. "The whole story is about modesty. Leave your family, leave what you know. Think of when God tells Abraham to follow what Sarah says in regard to Ishmael. We know Abraham felt bad about this; he had to send Ishmael away. But he knew he didn't understand everything.

"You can take the story of Abraham and teach people they don't have all the answers, because we **are** Abraham—just like all those commentators said—and we don't have all the answers. We don't know our destination. And we certainly don't know everything about God."

6

CHRISTIANS

THOUGH IT'S NOT YET 10:30 IN THE MORNING, the bishop of Jerusalem pours me a snifter of brandy. Then he brews me a cup of tea. Then he shows me a trick with his food. We are sitting in his crowded kitchen in the Old City, a few steps from the Holy Sepulcher, and he's fussing around like a talkative aunt. He takes a dried fig from a bowl, splits it in two, places a walnut in the middle of the flesh, then sandwiches the whole thing together and pops it into my mouth. "Isn't that fabulous!" he says. "I learned that from a monk in Lebanon."

Bishop Theophanes is a kitchen-table conjurer of sorts, a short, hearty Nathan Lane look-alike with a beard who could serve as the magician at a backyard birthday party but who happens to be the head of the Greek Orthodox Church in the holiest spot in Christendom. He controls half of the church where Jesus was crucified, he supervises the Golgotha itself, and he views himself as the spiritual heir of a line that stretches from Adam to today, with two pivotal stops along the way—Abraham and Jesus. Abraham is so important to the Greek Church that the chapel just above the Golgotha is called the Convent of Abraham.

"The greatness of our father Abraham is that he had a clear idea of God, clearer than other nations," he says.

I have come to talk about how Christians have viewed Abraham over the centuries. The Christian interpretation grew out of the Jewish one and for generations offered a similarly broad message, that Abraham's blessing was open to all people, regardless of lineage. But over time, just as Jews tried to claim Abraham uniquely, Christians attempted to commandeer Abraham for themselves. The deterioration of the relationship between Jews and Christians can be seen as vividly as anyplace else in their rivalry over their shared father.

"God talked to Abraham in the way he talks to other people, but we don't hear it," Bishop Theophanes continued. "We are not on the same level. But Abraham, at that happy moment for humanity, heard God's words. He understood that God was a figure you could talk to in an anthropomorphic way. It's very moving. Meeting God is something overwhelming, and Abraham did it first. He's the beginning of revelation. Spiritually speaking, he's the beginning of humanity."

"And is he the beginning of Christianity?"

He shook his head. "God's revelation traveled from Abraham to the prophets to Jesus. You can say that this revelation was meant only for Christians, but I don't think that way. There is a common psyche in the world in which humans lunge for the divine. That is God's imprint left on us, which all religious people feel. Abraham just felt it more clearly."

As best as anyone can tell, Jesus was likely born in the last years of the first millennium B.C.E. in Roman-controlled Palestine. Jesus (his actual name was Joshua) was born a Jew and died a Jew. He and his followers practiced circumcision, observed Passover, and followed the law. They were not out to found a new religion but, like the residents at Qumran and elsewhere, hoped to improve the existing one. Judaism, they claimed, had corrupted the Temple, abandoned the poor, and blasphemed the laws of purity.

But these problems could be mended with a

new leader. In the future, Jesus says in Matthew, "Many will come from east and west and will eat with Abraham, Isaac, and Jacob in the kingdom of heaven."

Many flocked to hear this new preacher, a development that aroused the suspicions of both the Jewish guardians of the Temple and the Roman authorities. Jesus was ultimately crucified for his crimes against the state, a distinctly Roman method of execution. But Jesus' story did not end there. If anything, his popularity ignited as his followers spread word that Jesus had not actually died irreparably on the cross. He was returned to life. Many began saying what Jesus himself had not claimed, which is that he was the messiah Jews had been awaiting for centuries. He was, as Paul called him, the "Son of God."

Jesus' followers—still Jews at the time—were so inspired by their belief that Jesus was the savior that they rushed to share the gospel. "Join us!" they shouted to their fellow believers. "The good news of the kingdom is proclaimed." Few Jews came. Perhaps the destruction of the Temple made them skittish. Perhaps they were blinded by habit. Perhaps they were unpersuaded. Whatever the reason, Jesus' disciples decided to broaden their appeal to include **non**-Jews. To do this, they needed to link Jesus to a figure who was not Jewish. They needed a founding father who was blessed by God, who had a deep spiritual pedigree, and who exemplified the faith that Jesus himself embodied.

They needed Abraham.

The first to realize this was Paul, the earliest apostle to write extensively about Jesus. Paul was a deeply believing Jew who came to believe in Jesus. He was bright, very logical, but not formally educated. He was a man of action who was aggressive and combative with his interlocutors. Paul dictated a series of letters that are named for the people he sent them to—Romans, Galatians, Corinthians—in which he addresses particular problems in each community and tries to lure believers to his cause. To help make his message more resonant with Jews in particular, he uses the techniques most familiar to his audience: rabbinic midrash. He retells the story of Abraham to emphasize what he thinks is most important.

In the fourteen letters of Paul included in the New Testament, Paul refers to Abraham a total of nineteen times, more than to any other figure except Jesus. Paul refers to Abraham more than twice as often as **all the prophets** in the latter half of the Hebrew Bible refer to him. We are clearly seeing an increase in Abraham's importance. Paul essentially chooses Abraham in the same way the rabbis chose him. Why?

First, Judaism was the dominant religion at the time, and Paul needed to define himself in terms that Jews could understand but also in terms that distinguished him from the Jews. Second, Paul wanted to sidestep what he viewed as the tyranny of the law in Jewish life. Finally, he desired a way to circumvent the tribal particularism of Judaism, the defining characteristic of which was that all men were required to be circumcised. In Paul's mind, these strands combined to limit Judaism, whereas he wanted to expand it by welcoming Gentiles through the gospel of Christ.

Abraham was the perfect model for Paul's new vision of Christ-enhanced Judaism, because Abraham developed a unique relationship with God before Judaism was invented, before the law was given, even before circumcision was prescribed. To prove his point, Paul turned to a line in Genesis 15. After Abraham arrives in the Promised Land and questions God's vow to give him a son, God reassures him by showing him the stars in heaven and saying his offspring will be just as uncountable. As the New Revised Standard Version describes the moment, in language more familiar to Christians, Abraham "believed the Lord; and the Lord reckoned it to him as righteousness."

For Paul, this is the key line in the Abraham story, and possibly the most important line in the entire Five Books of Moses. Abraham received recognition in God's eyes because he **believed** God, because he had **faith** that if he left his father's house and went forth as God asked he would become a great nation. "How then was it reckoned to him?" Paul asks in Romans 4:10. "Was it before or after he had been circumcised? It was not after, but before." This could mean only one thing: **Circumcision is not central to faith.**

Abraham's circumcision, which comes at least thirteen years later, is not a precondition for righteous behavior, Paul argued, it's a reward for it. For Paul, the purpose of circumcision was twofold. First, to make Abraham "the ancestor of all who believe without being circumcised," and second to make him "the ancestor of the circumcised." Abraham, in other words, is the father of Jews and Gentiles alike. Any person who shows faith is a descendant of Abraham.

Paul views faith as the keystone in Abraham's relationship with God. But faith for Paul is not blind observance; it's a dynamic, inner experience. As the Reverend Dr. Richard Wood, the former dean of Yale Divinity School, explained to me, "Paul is haunted with the sense of his own sin. In some ways the most profound thing he contributed to the history of Christian thought was his analysis of the nature of human evil. He says the fundamental problem we face is that, in our attempt to be righteous, pride sets in." Paul reads Abraham as someone who was blessed by God **even though** he was not righteous. And the reason: He had faith. "'That's it!' Paul says. If God will treat me as righteous in spite of my sin, then I display no pride. The initiative is all God's."

This is midrash at its most creative—and most elastic. As the Reverend Dr. Wood, a gregarious midwesterner and former president of Earlham College in Indiana, said, "He takes Genesis and does something questionable with it, in that he's using it to answer a question different than the author of Genesis had in mind." But Paul does not stop there. He goes further in Romans 4 to say that because Abraham received God's promise half a millennium before God delivered his law on Sinai, the law itself is not central to God's blessing. "If it is the adherents of the law who are to be heirs," Paul says, "faith is null and the promise is void."

Paul's minimization of the law is not inconsistent with Israelite history. Mosaic law was not central to the nation during the time of David and Solomon. But Paul's view did run counter to

Judaism in his time, which **was** built on the law. Paul goes around God's more detailed covenant with Moses in order to get back to his more general covenant with Abraham. "All who rely on the works of the law are under a curse," he says in Galatians 3. "My point is this, the law, which came four hundred thirty years later, does not annul a covenant previously ratified by God." God granted inheritance to Abraham through promise, not through legislation.

This point sets up Paul's climactic flourish. In Genesis, God promised his blessing to "Abraham and his offspring," he notes. **Offspring** in the text is singular, not plural. (Though Paul was writing in Greek, the same distinction holds.) "It does not say, 'And to offsprings,'" Paul notes. This means the promise of Abraham is actually intended not for many people, as Jews claim, but for one person. That one person is Christ. "If you belong to Christ, then you are Abraham's offspring, heirs according to promise." Jesus, Paul stresses, is the true descendant of Abraham, and people who accept him as their savior become members of Abraham's family, regardless of whether they are circumcised.

Paul's accomplishment here is masterful: He completely reinterprets the Hebrew Bible, not by abandoning the biblical story but by using it for his own purposes. He discards genealogy, which would appear to be a central focus of Genesis, and replaces it with faith. Biology is no longer important; lineage is passed down through belief, not through blood.

Moreover, Paul does this while claiming that he's still Jewish and that Jews who follow the law are still Abraham's descendants. The law, he explains, was merely added by God as a temporary measure because the Israelites had transgressed. They needed the law to guide them until pure faith returned. Jesus provided that faith. Paul goes on in Galatians 3 to say, "There is no longer Jew or Greek, there is no longer slave or free, there is no longer male and female; for all of you are one in Christ Jesus."

What Paul does here is exactly what the rabbis and philosophers of his time were doing: he creates a new Abraham for his own purposes. He deemphasizes the narrative dramas of Abraham's life—his arguing with God at Sodom and Gomorrah, his attempt to sacrifice his son—and focuses instead on the early, primal moment when he left his father's house and went forth into the unknown. And Paul does this, he stresses, to emphasize that Abraham was a vessel of God's universal grace.

Whether Paul's words actually are universal, or whether they subtly exclude Jews who don't believe in Christ, is a matter of debate. Paul, for his part, claims to be inclusive. "I ask then, has God rejected his people?" he says in Romans 11. "By no means! I myself am an Israelite, a descendant of Abraham." And, unlike his successors, Paul does not blame the Jews for Jesus' death or say God founded the church as a wrath against his people.

But he does vacillate, as when he says in Romans 11 that some Jews will be broken off the holy tree of life and the Gentiles, "a wild olive shoot," will be grafted in their place. "Paul's big problem," said Jon Levenson of Harvard, "is, How reliable is his God? Why should we believe this deity whose past promises to Abraham's children have proven false? From now on, whatever difficulties arise will be resolved through Christ. The Jews have been sawn off the tree."

Still, most observers agree that Paul was primarily trying to draw Gentiles into the family of Abraham rather than to keep Jews out. As the Reverend Dr. Wood explained, "Suppose you and I were in a Jewish congregation at the time, and we came to believe that indeed Jesus was the messiah. Would Paul expect us to stop practicing circumcision, or abandon the law? I don't think so. In fact, I think he'd be shocked at the idea. He's trying to make a bigger tent."

"So you think it's an inclusivist message?"

"I do."

"But what about the consequences of his argument?" I said. "I have a visceral response when I read these passages that while his message might be inclusivist, you can already see the machines of anti-Judaism turning."

"Absolutely," he said. "I can identify with that response. I didn't grow up thinking about it, because I didn't grow up thinking about that question. But you can see in Paul's more radical moments that he almost seems to condemn the law. In hindsight, when you look at the tragic history of the split between Judaism and Christianity over a two-thousand-year period and you read these passages, you say, 'Darn it, Paul! You've created huge problems without realizing it.'

"Because once you've got two rival groups toward the end of the first century, Paul has given the justification, I think quite unintentionally, for abandoning the good things in the Jewish tradition. And he's done this through the great patriarch of the Jewish tradition himself."

After about an hour in Bishop Theophanes' kitchen, he suggested we visit the church. He donned a black cape and a high black hat that looked like a top hat without the brim. When he stepped outside and led the way through his garden, I couldn't help thinking that he looked like the king on a chessboard.

Outside, the bustle around the entrance to the Holy Sepulcher parted as the bishop entered. Monks scurried over to greet him. A female worshiper darted forward, bowed on one knee, and kissed the top of his hand, uttering prayers. He greeted her for a few seconds, bowed, and gestured me behind a door I had never noticed before and into a stone stairwell.

Within seconds we were standing on the roof of the basilica. It was dimpled with the tops of domes and scarred with brick, plaster, and concrete from a hundred renovations and expansions. He led me into a chamber just large enough to hold a dozen people. The room, built in the fifteenth century, was encircled with frescoes. The images in the upper tier depicted events from the life of Jesus; the lower tier depicted scenes from the life of Abraham, including his near sacrifice of his son and his meeting the messengers of God on their way to Sodom and Gomorrah.

"Here is the place, according to tradition, where Abraham sacrificed his son," the bishop said, "and where God sacrificed Jesus. We are directly above the Golgotha. They bring simple people here and tell them this is the exact spot. For some people that's important."

"But not for you?"

"I don't care about archaeology. For me the allegory is more important. Everything in life has two natures, you see, the physical and the spiritual. In this wall there are two dimensions. In you there are two dimensions. In Abraham there are two dimensions, too."

I asked him what he meant.

"Abraham has God in him and humanity in him. He established the unity that reached its fulfillment in Jesus Christ."

"So Abraham is the tension between being human and being God."

"Not negative tension!" he said. "Positive tension. You can't separate being human and being godly." To illustrate, he began to explain the reason behind the chapel's depictions of Abraham and Jesus. The visitor enters on a human level and meets Abraham eye to eye, then lifts his eyes to Jesus, then lifts his eyes again toward heaven. Each visitor reexperiences the ascension to God.

"The important thing to remember about Abraham is that he lives in all of us. When we do the liturgy, we lay out the bread, which represents Jesus. Next to it we put another piece of bread, which represents Mary. Next to it we put nine smaller pieces that represent the nine altars of servants, apostles, prophets, and others. Abraham is one of the prophets. In front we put a small crumble that represents the people. All this we put into the chalice, with the Holy Spirit." He closed his eyes and waved his hands in the air to indicate the transformation. "And this becomes the body of Christ."

He opened his eyes and looked at me. "To me this crumble of bread is more important than the Bible. That's just a story that happened a long time ago. The liturgy happens every time we do it. For me, Abraham still lives in that chalice. And he lives in me."

"Does that mean he **doesn't** live in me?" I asked.

"He does live in you," he said. "Look, I'm not going to make excuses. What the Church did with Abraham was bitter and cruel. But a hundred years from now, the serious people will be considered ecumenical. They will understand that Abraham belongs to all humanity."

The idea that Abraham belongs to all humanity, which appears at least in spirit in the Letters of Paul, began to dissipate rapidly in early Christian writing. Abraham is a frequent though not dominant figure in the Gospels, the four accounts of Jesus' life that were written in the late first century C.E. The Gospels, along with Paul's Letters and various other writings, collectively make up the New Testament. Though the Gospels were written after Paul, they actually appear earlier in Christian Scripture under the names Matthew, Mark, Luke, and John. Abraham is important enough to appear in the **first sentence** of the New Testament, in the Gospel of Matthew: "An account of the genealogy of Jesus the Messiah, the son of David, the son of Abraham."

Unlike Paul, the Gospels pick up on the importance of genealogy in the Hebrew Bible and try to link Jesus directly with Abraham. Matthew ignores Ishmael, for instance, and says that Abraham was the father of Isaac, who was the father of Jacob, and on down the line. Matthew counts fourteen generations from Abraham to David, fourteen more from David to the deportation to Babylon, and fourteen more from Babylon to Christ. David almost certainly appears in this lineage because the prophet Micah said the Jewish messiah would come from his clan. Abraham most likely appears because Matthew wants to root Jesus as deep as possible in the soil of Israelite history and give him the prestige of antiquity.

The Gospels also find spiritual qualities of Jesus rooted in Abraham. In Luke 16, Jesus tells a parable about a rich man who dresses in purple and linen, and a poor man, Lazarus, who eats the crumbs of the rich man's table and has his sores licked by a dog. The rich man dies and goes to hell. The poor man dies and is "carried away by the angels to be with Abraham."

Even from his abyss, the rich man pleads with Abraham for mercy, but Abraham says, "No, in your lifetime you received your good things" and Lazarus evil things. "But now he is comforted here, and you are in agony." This passage shows clear debts to Jewish interpreters. It takes a contemporary Christian ideal—in this case, care for the downtrodden—and retroactively grounds it in the life of Abraham. Abraham, in other words, is being turned into Jesus.

This merging of Abraham and Jesus reaches a climax in the Gospel of John. The fourth Gospel is sometimes called the Gospel of Gospels because it was written later than the others, around 85 C.E., and effectively attempts to synthesize the prior three. John is also the most spiritual of the Gospels. The text is less interested in Jesus' humanity and more interested in his divinity. Jesus is always something other than human. He is the word of God incarnate in a historical person.

This image is vividly on display in an arresting—and controversial—parable. In John 8, Jesus is teaching a group of scribes and Jewish sectarians in the Temple. "I am the light of the world," he says. "Whoever follows me will never walk in darkness." The Jews resist, saying, "Your testimony is not valid." Jesus says they should not judge him by human standards because he was sent by God. If you follow me, he continues, "you will know the truth, and the truth will make you free."

But we are descendants of Abraham, the Jews counter, and "we have never been slaves to anyone." (They apparently overlook, or are unaware of, the period in Egypt.) "I know that you are descendants of Abraham," Jesus says, "yet you look for an opportunity to kill me, because there is no place in you for my word." He adds, "Whoever keeps my word will never see death." This incenses the Jews even more. "Now we know that you have a demon," the Jews reply. Abraham is dead. "Are you greater than our father Abraham?"

"Your ancestor rejoiced that he would see my day," Jesus replies. "He saw it and was glad." Suddenly Abraham knows the gospel thousands of years before Jesus was born.

The Jews reply with outrage: "You are not fifty years, and have you seen Abraham?"

And Jesus responds with one of the more contentious lines in the New Testament: "Very truly, I tell you, before Abraham was, I am."

The Jews react by picking up stones and hurling them at Jesus.

Jesus' statement at the end of John 8 is considered the clearest implication of his divinity in the Gospels. Jesus is now godlike in his ability to exist across time and space, and he expresses this by saying that he lived **before** Abraham. Jesus further suggests that he told Abraham who he was and that Abraham accepted. Jesus no longer supersedes Abraham; he **precedes** him. Jesus is not the seed of Abraham; Abraham is the seed of Christ.

The Jews, not surprisingly, reject this union and are likened to the devil. For this reason, many scholars consider this passage the most anti-Jewish in the entire New Testament. As the Reverend Dr. Wood said, "This is tough stuff. It's a theology of the end of the first century put into the mouth of Jesus. Would Jesus say that? I find it impossible to believe. It's just so out of character with most of the rest of what we have reason to think he said."

Still, as he pointed out, John does have Jesus saying it, and the consequences are immense. The Jews' response—throwing stones—captures their anger. The breach between Jews and Christians now seems irreparable. Dialogue has been replaced by fighting.

And why? From the Christian perspective, Jews deny Jesus his right to be considered divine. From the Jewish perspective, Jesus denies Jews—or at least the Jews he's arguing with—what for centuries has defined their identity: the right to be considered children of Abraham. As Jesus says during this argument, "If you were Abraham's children, you would be doing what Abraham did, but now you are trying to kill me." Without Abraham, the Jews have lost their connection to God. And, suddenly, Abraham is no longer the shared father of all humanity; he's the expression of the rift between Christians and Jews.

And what a rift it becomes.

In the centuries after the Gospels were recorded, early Church writers continued to extend the rivalry between Christians and Jews. As in other areas, the destruction of the Temple in the late first century C.E. proved pivotal. Church fathers saw in the misfortune of the Jews more evidence of their own triumph and a vindication for their claim to be the true kingdom of Israel.

The Church, which had been on the defensive toward Judaism, now went on the offensive.

Prominent writers such as Justin Martyr and Irenaeus (from the second century) and Eusebius (from the fourth) began to argue that Abraham wasn't Jewish after all but Christian. Justin, who was born in the town where Abraham first stopped in the Promised Land, was the first writer of any status to regard **all** Jews as enemies of Christ. Abraham, Justin claims, was actually called by Jesus in the same voice that summons all believers to Christ. As a result, Christians will inherit the Holy Land and are really "the nation promised to Abraham by God."

Now, not only have Jews been condemned by Jesus but they've actually been disinherited from the land and orphaned from God.

Irenaeus goes even further, saying that Christianity is not a new faith at all but the original faith, the one that brought Abraham to his righteousness. "The Lord was not unknown to Abraham, whose day he desired to see." In fact, it was through Christ, who appeared to Abraham in bodily form, that Abraham came to know God.

The final rupture came with Augustine. The fourth-century theologian argued that Jews blindly and shamelessly look at history through fleshly eyes, not spiritual ones. The proper way to view time, he insisted, is through the eyes of the eternal Son of God. To prove his point, he relied on the inflammatory passage in John 8 in which Jesus says, "Before Abraham was, I am." "Weigh the words, and get a knowledge of the mystery," he writes. Jesus does not say, "Before Abraham was, I was," because Jesus was **never made**. He simply **is**.

As a result, believers in Christ constitute the superior religion, Augustine stated. Just as God prefers the younger sons to the older ones in the Bible, so he prefers the younger religion, Christianity, to the older one, Judaism. Jews can continue to exist, but only because their tradition provides the dark light out of which the white light of Christian truth emerges. Judaism, in other words, now serves Christianity. Abraham has a new nation, the nation of Christ.

What John suggested and Justin reinforced, Augustine now locks into place for nearly fifteen hundred years of Christian history. Abraham, whom Paul called the "ancestor of all who believe," has now become the ancestor for all who hate. When Nazi propagandists were looking for justification for their anti-Semitism, for example, they cited works from this period. They went so far as to call Justin Martyr the "greatest anti-Semite of Christian antiquity."

Still, what these Christian interpreters did is remarkably similar to what Jewish interpreters did: They took a biblical figure open to all, tossed out what they wanted to ignore, ginned up what they wanted to stress, and ended up with a symbol for their own uniqueness that looked far more like a mirror image of their own fantasies than a reflection of the original story. Abraham is now a Christian, who knew Jesus, heard the gospel, and passed down God's blessing exclusively to those who embrace the body of Christ.

Jews, as well as other biological descendants of Abraham, and indeed anyone who rejects the good news of Christ, are dispossessed, dislodged, and left to wither in oblivion. Abraham, initially used to justify the inclusion of Gentiles in God's kingdom, is now used to certify the exclusion of Jews from their own heritage. Abraham may have stopped short of killing off his flesh and blood on Moriah, but Christians have now done it for him.

Once again, as an outsider encountering this hateful tradition, I was flummoxed. Abraham has been transformed so wildly by his own self-proclaimed descendants that he bears little resemblance to the portrait now left to fade in the

Bible. The biblical story itself may have been doctored over time; it may have been altered immeasurably. But it still manages to convey a more generous message of God's grace than does either of the portraits Abraham's supposed spiritual inheritors were busily creating.

Once more, I was left with a question: Why not reject these interpretations? Why not rebuff the Christian exclusive interpretation of Abraham as being as artificial as the Jewish one?

"Because you can't," said the Reverend Petra Heldt. The Reverend Ms. Heldt is a German Lutheran minister who heads the Ecumenical Theological Research Fraternity in Jerusalem. A petite woman with a wide, serene face and hair tucked in a bun, she was born in Berlin but moved to Israel in the 1970s to improve Jewish-Christian relations. When I met her in the library of her office, she was days away from finishing her Ph.D. on the use of Abraham in early Christian writing.

"Every story, the moment it's written down, will be reread," she said. "And every rereading will be a reinterpretation. In that sense, there is not an original story and there is not an original message."

As she spoke, she kept her hands tucked between her legs, as if not to draw too much attention to them. The reason is they are covered in grafts. In 1997 the Reverend Ms. Heldt was almost incinerated in a double suicide bombing in Jerusalem's Mahane Yehuda Market. She was shopping for dinner when she heard a bomb explode a few stalls away. As she started to run, she noticed her friend Nissim, a fishmonger, shaking hands with a Palestinian. But instead of releasing Nissim's hand, the man pulled him closer and detonated a second bomb. Another fireball erupted, sending her flying.

By the time she landed, second- and third-degree burns covered her body, and pieces of the bomb were lodged in her legs and feet. Half an hour later, as she arrived at Hadassah Hospital, where she would spend the next six weeks in the burn unit, her eyes swollen shut by the burns, unable to eat or drink, a reporter stuck a microphone in her face. "Why do you think you survived?"

Her answer was as miraculous as her survival: "To have an opportunity to speak about the greatness of God. We are his tools to bring reconciliation to this world."

"If you look at history," she told me, "each religion, at different times, for different reasons, tried to establish itself as the dominant religion. Claiming Abraham for yourself is just one way to establish your authority." This power grab usually occurs at historical turning points, she noted. For Jews it was after the Second Temple was destroyed and they had to buttress their sagging identity. For Christians it was after the fall of Rome in the fourth and fifth centuries, when they lost their political protection. "It's a psychological need triggered by political circumstances. You use your culture to establish your triumphalism because your political power may be waning. You want to show that you've **always been there.** Abraham is a great way to prove that."

Given this history of using Abraham for political purposes, I said, "Do you think he's a good vessel for reconciliation?"

"I think he's the best there is."

"Why?"

"You can put everything into that vessel you would like. He's open enough. He's broad enough. Shakespeare couldn't have thought of a better figure. He's planted in that space of the world, so he precedes all of us, he's therefore **with** all of us. He's not identified as being beautiful, or Jewish, or Christian, or black, or white, or whatnot, so you can put everything into him that you want.

"Also, he has this divine connection, which is wonderful, and all these divine promises, which are inspiring. You really can't think of anyone else. He's perfect."

"So you're suggesting that one reason he's a great figure is the lack of detail in Genesis."

"Exactly. And this is typical of a very good hero. Do you have a clear idea of Hamlet or Oedipus? No! Fairy tales provide great heroes. You don't know if they're old or young, have black hair or blue eyes. That's why everyone loves them."

"So can you say to Christians, for example, that they should go back to the original story of Genesis and there they'll find that hero?"

"No Christian can see the story of Genesis without Paul; no Jew can see it without the rabbis."

"So how do you find that hero if you have all these interpretations between you and him?" This is exactly the bog I kept stumbling into, and I became so agitated I leapt out of my chair. We were seated between two long library bookcases. I went to stand at the end of one case, about ten feet from the Reverend Ms. Heldt. "Okay, I'm here," I said. "I'm me. And you're Abraham. And there are **all these books** between me and you. How do I **find** you? If I start reading through all these books, once I find an interesting one I'm going to stop, stay there for a while, and get waylaid. How do I get around these books and get back to Abraham?"

"Very simple," she said. "Kick them."

"**Kick** them?"

"You can kick them away now because you know what you're doing."

"I'm confused." I returned to my seat.

"Look, you first have to recognize that there **are** all these books between you and me. Which is already quite something because most people don't know they're there. Second, you have to find a way to free yourself from this kind of exclusivist thinking, which you'll never do, but at least you should try as much as possible. Then, when you're finished, we'll come together—you're a Jew, I'm a Christian—we'll sit down and begin to draw a picture of Abraham. I'll say, 'What do you know?' You'll ask what I know, and we'll come up with some basic features: He's a man, he lives in the desert. And we start from there."

"And when we start from there, do we go back through those books?"

"Of course, you'll bring your books, I'll bring my books. But we try to be critical toward each other."

"And what do we have in the end?"

"A giant figure, who holds our joint expectations in his life, and whose character we both see as representing the best of ourselves. It's beautiful. And it can happen." She paused. A wry smile crept across her face. "Now let's find a Muslim. The three of us will do the same, and we're on the way to solving the problems of the world."

7

MUSLIMS

A few days after the last Friday of Ramadan I walk hurriedly through the drizzly streets of the Muslim Quarter in the heart of Jerusalem's Old City. The air is gray and the mood even grayer. I duck underneath a Mamluk bridge and step through a rarely used tunnel before arriving at a small stone staircase just steps from the Iron Gate to the Haram al-Sharif. Two Israeli guards are manning the entrance. They eye me suspiciously. Westerners don't make this walk. A woman steps out of the doorway with her laundry, catches sight of me, and quickly retreats and slams the door.

At the top of a narrow staircase I enter a small, whitewashed office, with a green-screen computer, a floor heater, a coffeemaker, and a copy of the multivolume **Encyclopedia of Islam**. The office belongs to Dr. Yusef Nadsheh, the head of the Department of Islamic Archaeology for the

Palestinian Authority and curator of the Dome of the Rock. We chat for a few minutes and share a cup of tea. He shows me a chart of all the crescent shapes atop minarets across Jerusalem.

Promptly at 10:45 A.M., a broad-shouldered man with a town-elder face and a businesslike manner walks through the door and greets me coolly but cordially. I offer him a seat next to me. He declines and sits down across the room.

Sheikh Yusef Abu Sneina is the imam of El-Aksa Mosque, one of the most vocal Islamic leaders in Jerusalem, and the one who delivered the fiery sermon I overheard on the last Friday of Ramadan. He has dark hair and a salt-and-pepper beard cut close to his face. His black eyebrows are sharply etched and remind me, against my will, of Ayatollah Khomeini's, but his eyes crinkle in a gentle way. He is young, only forty-three years old. He is also nervous. This is his first interview with a non-Muslim reporter.

"He is known for his knowledge of the Koran," Yusef Nadsheh had said of the imam before he arrived. "He knows it by heart, as well as the hadith." He was referring to accounts of what the prophet Muhammad said and did that were gathered in the centuries after his death and are considered the most reliable authority on his thinking. "He also speaks beautiful Arabic. He lived for five years in Medina, the center of Islamic learning."

Our conversation was stilted at first. I thanked the sheikh for taking the time to meet me, and asked a few questions about his life. His answers were perfunctory. In time I asked him about the importance of Abraham to Islam.

"Abraham is a major figure," he said, his voice stern, lecturing. "His descendants are like a spine along the generations. Among the twenty-five prophets in Islam, seventeen belong to the family of Abraham. And Abraham himself makes eighteen. Everything in Islam is bound to him."

I asked him why, of all the people in the world, God chose Abraham.

"God didn't just choose Abraham," he said. "He tested Abraham. Abraham had problems with the king who worshiped idols, he had problems with his wife, he was old before he had children, God asked him to sacrifice his son. And every time he **submitted** to God. He was completely devoted to God. This is an example we all have to follow."

In the Torah, I mentioned, Abraham does not always obey God. He converses with God. He even argues with God. I asked him if he felt the same way about Abraham in the Koran.

"Yes," he said, and cited the example of Abraham and the birds, a story that is not in the Bible. In sura 2, Abraham asks God for proof that he can raise the dead. "Have you no faith?" God asks. "Yes," Abraham says, "but just to reassure my heart." So God tells Abraham to take four birds, cut their bodies to pieces, and scatter them over the mountains. Then he tells Abraham to summon them home. "They will come swiftly to you," God assures him.

"So God showed the power he had, and Abraham believed him," Sheikh Abu Sneina said. "Therefore Abraham submitted himself to God."

"So was Abraham a Muslim?" I asked. This was one of the key questions I had come to explore. The Muslim decision to embrace Abraham was arguably even more remarkable than the Christian decision to embrace him. Islam emerged a full six centuries after Christianity, and at least a millennium after Judaism. Muhammad lived **twenty-five hundred years** after Abraham would have lived. And yet Muhammad followed the same course that Paul and early Christians did, and the same course that Ezra and early Jews did: He attached his spiritual message to the earliest prophet. Then, just like those forebears, early Muslims, having basked in the glory of the past, proceeded to claim that past as theirs alone.

"That depends on what you mean by Muslim,"

Sheikh Abu Sneina said. "If you take a Muslim to be anyone who submits himself to God, then Islam began with Adam, continued through Abraham, then all the prophets of Judaism and Christianity. But if you mean a Muslim is one who follows Islam, with the prophet Muhammad and all the interpretations, then that comes much later."

"So which definition do you prefer?" I asked.

"For me, Abraham submitted himself to Allah. He did everything for God. I don't know if he's like me, but I would like to be like him."

The idea that in the seventh century after Christ another religion would arise out of the Middle East, use the same basic narrative as Judaism and Christianity, then quickly **supplant** them in terms of political and religious power came as a shock to almost everyone—including Arabs.

But not to Muhammad. Nearly two centuries after the death of Augustine, when Christianity was just developing its most virulent strain of triumphalism, a new prophet arose in Mecca to deliver the Arabs to what he considered their rightful place in the history of salvation. In many ways, Muhammad seemed like an unlikely messenger: He was around forty, a well-to-do trader, married to an older woman, illiterate. He was hardly the profile of a revolutionary.

But Muhammad had learned a lot traveling the Arabian Peninsula, an area beset by feuding tribes. Because of its adverse location in the parched core of the Fertile Crescent, Arabia had not shared in the abundance of culture and power that a regular supply of water brought Mesopotamia, Egypt, or even the Promised Land. Bedouin tribes had no agricultural surplus, no need for a complex society, no spur for civilization. Two millennia after monotheists first overturned the idols of their fathers, Arabians were still polytheists.

But Arabia was changing. International trade routes and more complex financial transactions were bringing more money and sophistication to the peninsula, led by Muhammad's tribe, the Qurysh. With greater contact with the outside world, tales of the monotheistic prophets were now circulating widely. Muhammad's gift was to recognize this change—and to husband it. He didn't push too hard at first; he didn't try to evangelize too loudly. He just told his story, and couched it as a chauvinistic coming-of-age for Arabs, a sort of Revenge of the **Infertile** Crescent.

Key to his patriotic message was Muhammad's language. Anyone who travels to the Middle East today knows that Arabic is a mellifluous, poetic language. Particularly Arabs who spend any time in the desert speak whatever languages they're speaking—Arabic, English, French—with a grace and loftiness that is evanescent, inspiring, and occasionally maddening. Arabic is many things: concrete is not one of them. More often it's flowing, evolving, sculpted, like a dune.

And Muhammad, by all accounts, spoke an Arabic even more arresting in its power and mesmerizing in its beauty than anyone had heard at the time, and few have heard since. One reason the Koran continues to exert such influence is that the poetic language reproduced in its suras has a luxuriance attributable only to God. Partly as a result, more than a century of academic dismemberment has had much less impact on the Koran than it has on the Bible. Pious Muslims continue to see the Koran as the unfiltered word of God, which is one reason for the devotion it elicits. There is no third-person narrative in the Koran. God speaks directly in all of the text's six thousand two hundred verses.

Another key to Muhammad's message was that it came populated with figures already familiar to his listeners. Jesus, Moses, David, and others were becoming well known in Arabia, from the large population of Jewish and Christian traders settled in the peninsula. But for maximum effect, Muhammad needed to link his message to a prophet his audience could identify with. To do that, he needed someone similar to him, someone connected to Arabia itself, and someone also bringing a message of monotheism to a reluctant population of polytheists.

He needed Abraham.

Abraham is mentioned in twenty-five of the Koran's one hundred fourteen suras, with sura 14 named after him. And the predominant message about Abraham is that he was upright, submitted to God, and rejected idol worship. As sura 60 says, "You have a good example in Abraham." He said to his people, "We disown you and the idols which you worship besides God. We renounce you: enmity and hate shall reign between us until you believe in God only."

Once again, the starting point for Islam is remarkably similar to the starting point for Judaism and Christianity: **Have faith in God**. And one man best personifies that message. "Why Abraham to me is such an interesting figure," said Bill Graham, the Harvard Islamicist, "is that while we don't know **anything** about him historically, there is this Near Eastern tradition that somehow portrays him as a man of unimaginable, almost idiotic faith. A man who in the face of all rationality believes in God. And because of that he stands out in history—whether he's mythological or real—as **the** figure who somehow catches the imagination of all three traditions."

Like Christianity, Islam began by casting itself as broadly as possible. In the early years of Muhammad's preaching, while he lived in Mecca, along the southwest coast of Arabia, he was careful to stress that Abraham was a **universal** figure of faith. Jews, Christians, and Muslims were all People of the Book, Muhammad said, who believed in the same God. In fact, Muhammad fully expected Jews and Christians to follow his return to pure monotheism. "Be courteous when you argue with the People of the Book," sura 29 says. "Say: 'We believe in that which has been revealed to us and which was revealed to you. Our God and your God is one. To him we submit.'"

This closeness between Muhammad and the other faiths only strengthened when a group of tribes living in nearby Yathrib, including Jews, invited the prophet to mediate a dispute. The prophet readily agreed. Like Jesus, he had stirred up controversy among Meccan leaders with his message of social and spiritual equality. The local oligarchs, who profited from such inequality as well as from the annual pilgrimages Arabians made to pagan shrines in the city, were beginning to strike back. Muhammad's migration from Mecca in July 622, called the **hijira,** is so seminal that it marks year one in the Muslim calendar. Muslims date their history not from Muhammad's birth or death, or even from the year he began to recite the Koran. Time begins the year the prophet left his native land, went forth to another land, and gave birth to a community of believers. The echo of Abraham's Call is unmistakable.

Yathrib, later renamed Medina, was founded as a Jewish settlement, and ten thousand Jews still lived in the city. Muhammad worked closely with Jewish leaders, enhanced his knowledge of the Bible, and adjusted his new religion to accommodate his allies even more. He set his weekly prayer day on Friday, so it would coincide with the time Jews were preparing for their Sabbath (and not compete with the Jewish workweek, as the Christian Sabbath did). In addition, he urged his worshipers to pray toward Jerusalem and declared that the Jewish Day of Atonement would also be a fasting day for Muslims.

But the warm relations between Jews and Muslims did not last. While the Jews may have been prepared to align politically with Muhammad, they were not prepared to accept him as a prophet. For Jews, the days of God's revelation had ended. The Koran suggests the prophet was frustrated by their reluctance. The tone of the suras that describe revelations received during this period is sometimes harsher than that of earlier ones, particularly toward Jews and Christians.

In sura 5, Allah says: "The Jews and the Christians say: 'We are the children of God and his loved ones.' Say: 'Why then does he punish you for your sins?'" The sura goes on to accuse the People of the Book of hiding certain things in their Scripture and delivers a pointed message to Christians. "Unbelievers are those who declare: 'God is the Messiah, the son of Mary.'" The passage ends: "Our apostle has come to you with revelations after an interval which saw no apostles, lest you say: 'No one has come to give us good news or to warn us.' Now someone has come to give you good news and to warn you. God has power over all things."

Gradually a schism began to develop between early Muslims on one side, Jews and Christians on the other. The process mirrored what happened between early Christians and Jews, when the new believers offered what they considered a universal message but the established believers failed to embrace it. In both cases, the new religion proceeded on its own.

In January 624 Muhammad introduced a monumental change: He asked his worshipers to turn around, to no longer face Jerusalem during their prayers but to face Mecca instead. Mecca was the original home of monotheism, the Koran says, and the previous direction had been only a test to know Muhammad's true adherents. From now on, Muslim worshipers would face the prophet's birthplace.

While this shift certainly widened the rupture among the religions, it did little to change the importance of Abraham. If anything, Abraham became even more important to Muslims as a symbol that true submission to God predated Judaism and Christianity. As sura 2 says, "They say: 'Accept the Jewish or the Christian faith and you shall be rightly guided.' Say: 'By no means! We believe in the faith of Abraham, the upright one.' " This faith was revealed not only to Abraham but also to "Ishmael, Isaac, Jacob, and the tribes; to Moses and Jesus and the other prophets." Islam, in other words, is the true universal faith.

Peace-loving Muslims point out that the Koran never advocates violence toward the other religions and never insisted Jews and Christians become Muslim. As Sheikh Feisal Abdul Rauf, of New York's Masjid al-Farah Mosque, told me, "The Koran is explicit. 'There shall be no compulsion in religion.' Faith has to be a matter of individual conscience. Even in places where Muslims were ruling over non-Muslims they never coerced them to convert."

But most scholars believe the split that took place in Medina is reflected in the text. As Bill Graham said, "If you take the Koran over time, there is an increasing challenging of Jews and Christians to respond now to God speaking again. And finally there's even a condemning of them after one contretemps or another. Then you get to the point where certain actions by the People of the Book were used as pretexts for persecution."

The most egregious example of this violent tendency occurred over the next three years as Muhammad, now with greater political clout, slowly banished those Jewish tribes in Medina that had turned against him and begun supporting his Meccan oppressors. Ultimately, Muhammad's followers slaughtered an estimated seven hundred Jews and sold their women and children into slavery. Any hope of a long-term alliance of faith was shattered. The new Muslims were now powerful enough to survive on their own.

After protracted struggle, Muhammad, in 628, made an alliance with the oligarchs of Mecca who had opposed him and marched into the city unopposed. By the year of his death, 632, he controlled all of Arabia. Monotheism had a new member religion; Abraham had a new address.

After I'd spent about a half hour with Sheikh Abu Sneina, the mood began to lighten somewhat. He still hadn't taken off his coat, but he had set down his briefcase. A couple of times he interrupted my questioning to point out that he had a few more things to say. One time I did the same to him, and we both laughed. Finally he seemed comfortable enough for me to ask him about the **Hajj.**

When Muhammad arrived back in Mecca, he began to purify the holy city of its polytheism and transform it into the capital of the new faith. He destroyed all the sanctuaries of paganism, except for one, the Ka'ba. Mecca had been a center of pilgrimage for generations, with the Ka'ba, the large black cube roughly forty feet in every direction, being the most prominent destination.

The Koran says the Ka'ba was actually built by Adam, then **rebuilt** by Abraham. During Noah's

Flood, the Ka'ba had been taken up to heaven, where angels fluttered around it, the origin of the tradition of pilgrims circumambulating the cube. Later, it was returned to earth and lost under the sands. During one of Abraham's visits to Arabia, a two-headed wind revealed the secret location, and Abraham set about reconstructing the primordial temple where God left his footprint on earth. When Abraham tired, Ishmael helped him by bringing a large rock to stand on; it came to be known as the Maqam Ibrahim for the footprint Abraham left on it.

Some interpreters note that Abraham and Ishmael did not entirely get along during this period. In some traditions, Ishmael could not find a cornerstone or was too late or too lazy to be of any help. His father says, "God would not entrust such a thing to you, my boy!"

After Abraham finished building the Ka'ba, God commanded him to go to the top of a nearby hill and summon all humankind to make a pilgrimage to the site. His voice was amplified so it could be heard around the world. Muhammad echoed Abraham's faithfulness when he once again called Muslims to make the same pilgrimage.

The pilgrimage, or **Hajj,** soon became one of the five pillars of Islam and one of the enduring reasons for Abraham's central role in the faith. All pilgrims—men and women—purify themselves, donning seamless white garments, and wearing strapless white shoes. They enter the Grand Mosque, where the Ka'ba is located, move clockwise around it seven times, then pray in the spot where Abraham stood. In subsequent events of the weeklong pilgrimage, worshipers run between the knolls of Safa and Marwa in commemoration of Hagar's frantic search for water for Ishmael and stone the pillars that represent the devil who tried to tempt Abraham to ignore God's command to sacrifice his son.

Unlike Jews or Christians, for whom he is a largely literary figure, for Muslims Abraham is a tangible figure intimately connected to one of the most moving experiences of their lives. As Sheikh Abu Sneina said when I asked him what feeling he got when he viewed the Ka'ba, "You get the sense that it was done to perfection. God instructed Abraham to build it, and he built it stone by stone, and he did it perfectly."

Sheikh Abu Sneina has made the pilgrimage five times. In honor of his completing the journey, he earned the right to put the name **Hajj** before his name. During our talk, Dr. Nadsheh referred to him as **Hajji** Yusef.

"When you walk around the Ka'ba you get the feeling that Allah tested Abraham," the imam continued, "and that Abraham survived and performed well in those tests. Then you stop and make two prayers. That's when you really feel closest to Abraham. It's very moving."

"What kind of feeling do you get?" I asked.

"It's a feeling of connection. You feel that you have a sort of channel between you and God. A spiritual feeling that you are human, but you are not human. You're human with a special capability because you are so close to God."

"And what do you want from Abraham at that moment?"

"You don't want anything from Abraham. You want things from God. Every time Abraham spoke to God, he never asked for something for himself. He always asked for his family. He was not selfish in that way, so we try not to be selfish either."

"Do you cry?"

"Some people cry loudly, because they're in pain. Some people cry quietly. Some people cry because they are sinful and their sins have been revealed. Some people cry out of joy."

"Did you cry?"

"Many times."

"What kind of tears?"

"Tears of worship."

Like Christianity, Islam spread rapidly in its first decades. Within a hundred years of the prophet's death in 632, under the first four caliphs, or rulers, and the first great dynasty (the Umayyads), Islam spread through Arabia, Syria, Palestine, Egypt, Persia, and much of Afghanistan as far as India, as well as across the whole of North Africa from Alexandria to Tunis. Also like Christianity, Islam quickly proved itself portable, adaptable, and inspirational to populations far removed from its historic and geographic epicenter. The long-promised great nation of Ishmael had finally come to be.

The long-repressed rivalry between Ishmael and Isaac was about to resurface.

In yet another similarity with Christianity, once Islam began to grow in stature and power, Muslim leaders started to distance themselves more aggressively from their monotheistic forebears. Islamic midrash, known as **tafsir,** is considered harsher toward Jews than toward Christians, largely because of the political circumstances during the prophet's lifetime. As one ninth-century commentator wrote, Muslims prefer Christians to Jews because the latter actively opposed the prophet in Medina: "The reason that the Christians are less hideous—though they certainly are ugly—is that the Israelite marries only another Israelite, and all of their conformity is brought back among them and confined with them . . . they have, therefore, not been distinguished either for their intelligence, their physique, or their cleverness."

Once again, a by-product of this process was that interpreters of the new religion expressed their feelings of superiority toward their monotheistic ancestors by attempting to tighten their claim on Abraham. For example, Muslim interpreters added a new twist to the construction of the Ka'ba. They pointed out that the spot was the one where the angel of God revealed a spring to Hagar, thereby saving Ishmael's life.

A more visible example of this growing grip over Abraham involves Muhammad's night journey. Sura 17 tells that God called Muhammad to make a night journey from the temple of Mecca to the "farther temple whose surroundings we have blessed." Interpreters elaborated to say that while Muhammad was sleeping at the Ka'ba, the angel Gabriel woke him and mounted him on the miraculous beast Buraq, who carried him to Jerusalem. There he met and prayed with "God's friend Abraham," as well as Moses, Jesus, and other prophets. A ladder then appeared and Muhammad ascended to heaven.

In heaven, Muhammad once again met various prophets, including Moses, "a man of dark color, great build, and a crooked nose." In the seventh level of heaven, Muhammad saw a man of mature age sitting on a chair at the gate of paradise. "I never saw a man who more resembled me," Muhammad said. "And Gabriel said: this is your ancestor Abraham." Muhammad no longer just emulates Abraham; he now **resembles** him. The link between them is not just spiritual, or even ancestral, it's physical.

The familiar wheel is beginning to turn again. Abraham is moving from being considered a universal figure open to all religions to being considered a more exclusive figure who favors one faith. Islam is beginning to put itself in the position toward its monotheistic forebears that Christianity earlier put itself in toward Jews. We understand the **true** faith of Abraham that you somehow corrupted, Muslims suggest, therefore we have replaced you in God's eyes.

Once again, interpreters found lines that supported their case in the Koran. Sura 3, for example, says, "The only true faith in God's sight is Islam. Those to whom the Scriptures were given disagreed among themselves, through insolence, only after knowledge had been vouchsafed them. He that denies God's revelations should know that swift is God's reckoning." For Muslims, the message of passages like this became clearer with time: Islam didn't supersede Christianity and Judaism, it **preceded** them. Islam, in fact, was the faith of Abraham, which his descendants twisted for their own purposes. Put another way: Before Abraham was, Islam am.

It was during this period, beginning around the tenth century and continuing for several hundred years, that Islam was at its political and cultural peak, dominating the world from the Indian Subcontinent to the Caucasus, from Central Asia into Southern and Central Europe. Many of the apparent conflicts among the religions were forged during this time, including the idea that Ishmael was the son Abraham was called to sacrifice. When I asked Sheikh Abu Sneina which of Abraham's sons was involved in the dream of sacrifice, he said Ishmael, and proceeded to lay out all the arguments.

"So this is a situation where the Bible is wrong?" I asked.

"Yes," he said.

Muslim superiority toward Jews and Christians eventually entered the political realm. In some places non-Muslims were ghettoized, forced to ride asses instead of horses, obliged to ride sidesaddle instead of astride, and even prevented from going out of doors when it rained or snowed lest their contaminants spread. As early as the ninth century, Christians and Jews in Baghdad were obliged to wear yellow emblems on their clothes, the origin of the yellow badge later used by the Nazis against Jews.

The great historian of Islam, Bernard Lewis, has written that Muslim discrimination against nonbelievers, while profound, never reached the levels of Christian hostility to Jews. "On the whole, in contrast to Christian anti-Semitism," he wrote in **The Jews of Islam,** "the Muslim attitude toward non-Muslims is one not of hate or fear or envy but simply of contempt."

This mind-set changed in the twentieth century with the struggles over European colonization in the Middle East, the emergence of the State of Israel, and the rise of American hegemony. These political battles gradually began to infect the religious dialogue, so that even a conversation about Abraham among Jews, Christians, and Muslims today often deteriorates into a disagreement about Jerusalem, Palestine, Osama bin Laden, Jewish settlements, suicide bombers, Iraqi schoolchildren, Iranian hostages, the Gulf War, Jewish control of the media, the Saudi royal family, the CIA, the Mossad.

And, inevitably, the will of God.

The night before I went to see Sheikh Abu Sneina, I met a Palestinian friend at a hotel in

Jerusalem, piled into the back of his beaten-up sedan, and headed deep into East Jerusalem to meet the imam of his local mosque. I had discussed Abraham with my friend, a tour guide and amateur archaeologist, and he offered to introduce me to his neighborhood cleric. "My brother studies with him every week," my friend said.

Masoud El Fassed was sitting in elegant robes on a small sofa in a shiny living room with white linoleum floors. He had a short white beard and wore an embroidered skullcap. His manner was gracious, if distant. He was not eager to answer questions about his background, even though his English was eloquent from years in London. When my friend and his brother served us teacups filled with warm, sweet yoghurt, walnuts, and cinnamon, we paused to enjoy what seemed like the best thing I had ever tasted in the Middle East.

Our conversation began in the ordinary way, as we talked about Abraham in the Bible and the Koran, his building of the Ka'ba, his night journey to Jerusalem. But when the topic turned to the sacrifice, the imam's tone shifted, as he began to suggest that Isaac was inferior to Ishmael. In the Bible, he said, even the prophets denounce the behavior of the Jews because they ignore the word of God. "Moses said it. David said it.

Malachi said it," he mentioned. "They all said that if the Jews don't follow the will of God they will wreak God's revenge. All the problems started with Isaac."

"So from your point of view God prefers Ishmael over Isaac?" I said.

"God does not prefer so-and-so," he said. "He prefers the people who worship him correctly."

"And the descendants of Ishmael worship him correctly?"

"Look at the Muslim nation," he said, "look around the whole world. We worship God around the clock, five times a day, then do extra prayers. Look at the Jews and Christians, you don't worship God as Muslims do."

"So what will happen to the descendants of Isaac who pray incorrectly?" I asked.

"God gives you the opportunity to submit yourselves to him and follow the rule of God. But you ignore him because you have become strong. You can deliver your message around the world, you can switch the mind of the people. You do the opposite of what God wants. You open banks, sexual places, gambling. Evil things. God gives you many chances, but of course we know that you're not going to follow.

"And look at what **happened,**" he continued, his voice animated but hardly hostile. "He sent people very strong, who killed themselves, in order to kill you. This is something unbelievable what happened in America, but it came from God."

At this point I was taken aback by his words but not outraged. I stayed calm, trying to follow his line of thought. I looked across the room. My friend was sinking in his chair, but his older brother was sitting erect, his eyes wide, his head nodding approvingly. He held the shoulders of his four-year-old son, making sure he faced the imam. The boy was rapt.

"So let me make sure I understand you correctly," I said. "You're saying that if I'm a Jew, and I'm a descendant of Abraham, Isaac, and Jacob, and I follow the laws of the Torah and I'm not following the **true laws** of Abraham and the Creator, then I'm going to be punished?"

"According to your Bible, yes. According to the Koran, yes. And the reason is because you abhor Islam and try to destroy the religion of the Creator. By forcing your ideas and way of thinking on the world, you show your hatred for God. Now you must follow the last prophet he sent. And then you'll be saved."

"So what will happen to me?" I asked. I was looking directly at him.

He looked directly back. "You'll die."

I couldn't think of anything to say.

"The punishment is going to come from the Creator," he continued, "but of course through the people. Like Hitler, for instance. According to the Jews, Hitler killed six million people. I was asking myself, 'Why does Hitler love the Jews so much that he grilled them alive?' I understood why when I studied the Bible. The Jews don't do what the Creator wants. They do the opposite."

At this point it was clear that our conversation was over, and I began to wonder how exactly I would get home. Was I being set up somehow? Was this a misunderstanding? Or was this just casual after-dinner discussion in East Jerusalem, with tea, crumpets, and chitchat about genocide? I had to ask another question.

There's a conversation going on in the world, I mentioned, among people of different faiths, who are attempting to see if they can get along, live side by side. "Can they?"

"We are Muslims," he said. "And this is Muslim land. If you want to live among us, what you believe is your problem. This is the message of God. Read it in the Bible, read it in the Koran."

"So there's no message of hope, not even in Abraham?"

"Usually that message comes from people who

do not believe in God. Abraham is the father of one religion, and that religion is Islam."

I did get home safely that night, riding silently back in the car with my friend. I craved a shower. The whole encounter left me rattled, and sad. I immediately wanted to forget it, pretend it didn't happen. Who was this guy who wouldn't tell me two things about himself? Was he a religious figure at all? Or was he just an agitator?

"It doesn't matter," said a journalist friend who writes a lot about religion in the region. "The unfortunate truth is that he represents the mainstream in Islam at the moment. You can find Jews who have a similar message of Jewish nationalism, but not that many. You can find apocalyptic Christians, but still a limited number. Your imam represents the bulk of Muslims, at least around here."

Because of my experience in East Jerusalem, I waited about an hour into my conversation with Sheikh Abu Sneina the following day before broaching the subject of politics. The sheikh was also known as something of a flamethrower. He would not be giving the closing sermon of Ramadan at El-Aksa unless he was prepared to use the platform of the third holiest mosque in Islam to rouse Palestinian hostility toward Israel. "Muslim Palestine is one and cannot be divided," he had said in a recent sermon. "Palestine is **waqf** land, part of the religious trust that belongs to Muslims throughout the world. No one has the right to give it up. Whoever does is a traitor to the trust and is nothing but a criminal whose end shall be in hell."

As our meeting was drawing to a close, I mentioned the interfaith conversation in the world and asked whether he believed Abraham was a uniting figure or a dividing figure.

"If Muslims, Jews, and Christians follow what is mentioned in the Koran, then Abraham can be a uniting figure," he said, and I felt we might be heading down a path similar to that of the night before. "But even if Jews and Christians just follow what's mentioned about Abraham in the Bible, then we can reach unity."

Now this was a new idea. "But we have two different texts," I said.

"But the principle is the same," he said. "You have a true heart, you have to believe there is one God. Maybe we have different approaches, but the destination is the same."

This was so radical in its openness that I didn't quite believe it at first. I mentioned that the previous Friday I had stood on a perch overlooking El-Aksa as he spoke. I could see Jews praying, Muslims praying, all the churches with their bells ringing. "And everybody could hear everybody else."

He laughed. "So what is your question?"

"Was that the sound of conflict or the sound of peace?"

"As Muslims we have the order to pray, to believe according to Islam, and God asks us very clearly to protest against other groups who have other beliefs. We want to spread Islam, to have a **jihad.** But that doesn't mean we have to fight. **Jihad** does not mean to fight people, it means to invite people to Islam, which is highly misunderstood, both historically and now. But this can be done peacefully."

"I would like to believe that," I said. "But people are dying. I live in New York."

"The situation is very difficult. There are problems in Palestinian society. People are deprived from coming to El-Aksa. Every family knows people who are prisoners, or who were killed. This political domination threatens religious tolerance. So religion is mixed with politics, you see."

"So when I look at the situation, should I feel sad, or concerned? Or should I feel that in the future the spirit of Abraham can prevail?"

"You should feel sadness," the imam said, "not just for the Muslim world but also for Jews and Christians."

We nodded.

"But despite this sadness," he continued, "hope must endure. We all sacrifice. We all have people killed. It's the same for Palestinians and Israelis, for Christians and Jews, for Americans, for people all over the world. We must find a way."

For the first time all morning I felt the imam emerging from his defensive posture. He was sitting on the edge of his chair now. His arms were stretching wide, his hands upstretched. His eyes burned. He was a preacher. He was a leader.

I lifted my voice in response. I moved to the edge of my chair, too. I swung my arms out wide. "So I give you a microphone," I said. "You can speak to the whole world. And I ask you to speak about Abraham. What is your message?"

We were sitting face-to-face now. The gap between us had disappeared. "Abraham was a man of faith," he began. "He worshiped God, and was thankful for God. He invented monotheism. He had high values. If all people—not just Muslims, Christians, Jews—follow the correct path of Abraham, I'm sure life would be better. But we are not doing that. The situation we are facing is that people are living their daily lives far away from the truly faithful, and from Abraham. If we look beyond the details, which we may disagree about, and follow the **principles** of Abraham—truth, morality, and coexistence—then most of our problems will disappear."

He finished with a rousing flourish of his hands and immediately stood up. I stood up, too, and we shook hands. I felt the impulse to embrace him but stopped short. The imam of El-Aksa, who had **memorized** the Koran and all the sayings of the prophets, had proclaimed that we could look beyond the details and focus on the principles. It seemed like enough of an embrace.

Out on the street a few minutes later, I stood by myself. The guards had disappeared. The rain had stopped. The sun was pushing through the clouds. I didn't quite know what to do. Part of me wanted to alert the media and tell them what I had heard: FIREBRAND IMAM DELIVERS A SERMON OF RECONCILIATION: "IGNORE THE DETAILS, EMBRACE ABRAHAM." Part of me wanted to call the peace negotiators.

Mostly I just wanted to believe.

So I slung my backpack over my shoulder. I turned my back to the Haram al-Sharif. And I walked.

BLOOD OF ABRAHAM

8

LEGACY

THE MOUNTAIN HIGH ROAD THAT LEADS south from Jerusalem toward Beer-sheba was once called the Patriarchs' Road, because it's the route the biblical forefathers took from the Galilee to the Negev. Abraham took this road on his first trek through the Promised Land, from Shechem to Bethel and down to Egypt. In recent years, the same route was called the Tunnel Road, because it contains the two longest tunnels in Israel. These days, the route is called the Blood Road, because it's the main target of Israeli and Palestinian snipers boring down from rival hills.

On a bitter, brilliant Thursday morning I set out on this road toward Hebron, one of the deadliest cities on the planet, the epicenter of Muslim-Jewish warfare, and the one place that most contains the echoes—and possibly the glimmers—of reconciliation. All three faiths agree Abraham bought land here, buried Sarah here, and was buried himself here. A building constructed over their burial caves two thousand years ago contains memorials to Abraham and Sarah, as well as to Isaac and Rebekah, Jacob and Leah. Jews, Christians, and Muslims have struggled for control of the site for generations.

Some have been willing to kill for it. Hebron, about twenty-five miles south of Jerusalem, was long a benchmark of coexistence; Jews and Muslims lived peacefully here for centuries and prayed together at the tombs (though Jews were restricted to the seventh step outside the building and were denied entrance). In Arabic the town is called El Khalil, or "the friend," the same name the Koran gives to Abraham. The name in Hebrew is Hevron, a derivative of **haver,** which also means "friend."

But for the last century the town has become a symbol of fanaticism. Riots in 1929, followed by decades of skirmishes, a massacre in 1994, and round-the-clock sniper fire, booby-trap bombs, and drive-by shootings have left the final resting place of Abraham a gory, embroiled, unrestful hive. The larger area is even worse. Just the night before I went, the Israeli military raided a Palestinian home in the city. A suspected Islamic militant fled into the night, and the soldiers shot and killed him. The story was so routine it didn't even make the front page of the papers.

"Aren't you nervous?" I asked my Palestinian friend Nasser, a Jerusalemite and cabdriver who agreed to shuttle me the one hour south to Hebron. In his late twenties with a veteran's sly nose for bridging the hostility between East and West, he was calm, even laconic, as he picked me up and turned down the hill toward the first tunnel, just minutes from the Old City.

"No," he said. "Actually, it's something most Muslims feel. I believe if I'm going to die—or be shot—it's my destiny. God wants me to die at this moment. Even if I'm at home, then I'll die. So why should I be afraid to go to dangerous places? This is what helps suicide bombers kill themselves. They believe it's their destiny."

"So you have no choice?"

"Correct. There are three things in Islam you have no control over: your money, your marriage, and your death. These are things that are determined by God."

He added, perhaps to calm me down, "Also, they don't really shoot at taxis, because they know taxis are driven by Palestinians. They usually know which cars have Jews in them."

His words didn't have the intended effect. The

road was empty, and chilling. Thirty-foot-high concrete barriers had been placed on either side of the bridge between the two tunnels in an attempt to shield the cars. The gray slabs were pocked with bullet holes from M-5-00 pump guns. Up on the sand-colored rocky hills to the east, dappled with vineyards and olive trees, a small cluster of buildings had perfect views of the road. "They usually shoot from unfinished buildings," Nasser said of the Palestinians.

After about twenty minutes we arrived at a checkpoint. "This could take a while," he said. The Israeli soldiers poked at the car a bit, stuck a mirror underneath the chassis, asked for our papers, and generally grumbled at us. After a few minutes they let us continue.

But we were hardly finished. We endured **five** more checkpoints in the next forty-five minutes. Some we passed through quickly, others slowly. A few had tanks along with the machine guns. A dispiriting glumness settled in, lifted only by the sun and blue sky. The juxtaposition of the tension and brilliant blue skies reminded me of being in New York on September 11. At several checkpoints, the soldiers asked where I was from. Ah—they nodded—you know what it's like. And then they waved us through.

"So if God has determined when you're going

to live and when you're going to die," I said as we made our way through the stony hills and valleys, "why not be a suicide bomber?"

"Suicide bombers want to be martyrs," he said. "They're very pious Muslims and believe they will get better places in Paradise. I am totally against killing civilians. The prophet Muhammad's first orders to his soldiers were 'Never kill a child, never kill a woman, never kill an old man, and never cut down a green tree.' But now the imams say we're in a different situation. We have no weapons to defend ourselves so killing is the only way. It's good for Islam, they say."

Perhaps the most surprising aspect of my search for Abraham was how utterly different it was from what I'd expected. The first shock, of course, was discovering that there was not a single Abraham but a myriad of rival Abrahams. But an even greater surprise was discovering that none of the faith leaders I talked to about this seemingly intractable morass was all that concerned. With a few isolated exceptions, **every conversation** I had about Abraham—with Jews, Christians, and Muslims alike—ended with a formula for balancing these competing Abrahams into a workable dialogue.

Abraham clearly provided a road map of what had gone wrong among the religions. Could he also provide a road map for how to make it right?

Something was clearly going on in the world. But what?

My journey had one final leg.

The idea that the monotheistic religions could relate to one another as equals without trying to subvert or destroy one another would have seemed unthinkable a century ago. The notion that they might actually talk to one another about shared ideals would have been a fantasy worthy of Jules Verne. At the end of the nineteenth century the struggle among the three monotheistic religions seemed to be reaching something of a resolution—and it wasn't one of parity.

Judaism, for starters, would be a minor religion, with no homeland and almost no political clout. Jews were still chosen, the rabbis said; they alone must follow God's strict laws; but they did so, in part, so that God would bless all humanity through them, as he did through Abraham. This belief is more elitism than triumphalism and, as distasteful as it might seem, it would prove far less aggressive toward others.

Islam, meanwhile, had also come up short in its

bid for triumphal domination. Islam never tried to eradicate Judaism and Christianity, but Islamic states did aggressively try to conquer the world and institute their own theocracy. In the Middle Ages this effort set up a battle between Christendom and Islam, two behemoths with political aspirations. Islam nearly won, getting as far as the gates of Vienna in 1529, before stalling. By the end of the nineteenth century, Islam had retreated back to the sands, an echo of its former self.

Christianity, meanwhile, was ascendant, in part because it adapted to the modern world. Islam may have failed in its attack on Christianity, but Martin Luther didn't. The Reformation, coming on the tail of the Renaissance, began the long process of dismantling the Church's exclusive claim to divine salvation. The Enlightenment dampened this avowal even further, as much of Western Europe and America embraced liberal notions of secular, democratic political institutions with religious tolerance at least nominally at their heart.

Still, even with its **political** power splintered, Christianity as a religion seemed stronger than ever in the eighteenth and nineteenth centuries. Christians dominated Europe, and through imperialism extended their cultural influence to

North America, South America, much of Africa, and parts of Asia and the Middle East. Viewed in terms of the religious wars of the previous millennium, Christianity seemed to have triumphed.

The twentieth century shattered this illusion. Two world wars, the end of colonialism, and the rise of cultural self-expression around the world dented all dreams that Christianity could simply seize control of salvation forever. Other religions came charging back. Judaism, long ghettoized around the world and nearly eliminated in Central Europe, even regained control of its spiritual heart, Jerusalem, as well as much of the land promised to Abraham, which it had not occupied for nineteen centuries.

Islam also surged to greater prominence. The combustible engine of modernism, which had propelled the West to far greater power than the Islamic world, turned out to run most efficiently on Middle Eastern oil. Civilization, which had begun in the Fertile Crescent and largely shunned the desert, suddenly needed the desert for its survival. Even agriculture depended on the fruit of the sands. This turnabout brought new power to the Middle East and gave a boost to fledgling Islamic regimes—Iran, Iraq, Saudi Arabia—just throwing off European imperialists. From North Africa to Southeast Asia, Islam regained a base of power.

At the start of the twenty-first century, the idea that one religion was going to extinguish the others was deader than it had been in two thousand years—and possibly ever. The battle for God was approaching stalemate. A new type of religious interaction was needed, involving not just swords, plowshares, and the idea of triumph but conversation, interaction, and the idea of pluralism. As the Reverend Dr. Richard Wood, late of Yale, said, "What's happened, at least in theological circles, is that triumphalism is dead. People aren't even asking the question. Of course there are a bunch of people who haven't figured this out yet. But they will."

Fourteen hundred years after the rise of Muhammad, two thousand years after the ascent of Christianity, twenty-five hundred years after the origin of Judaism, and **four thousand** years after the birth of Abraham, the three monotheistic religions were inching toward a posture of open—and **equal**—deliberation. This state of affairs set up a new question for the faiths to ponder: Can the children of Abraham actually coexist?

After six checkpoints and nearly an hour, Nasser and I approached the large yellow metal gate at the entrance to Kiryat Arba, the besieged Jewish settlement just up the hill from the Palestinian-controlled heart of Hebron. Kiryat Arba has a population of six thousand, Hebron proper a population of one hundred thousand. As a result, Kiryat Arba is one of the most highly guarded outposts in the entire West Bank.

An Israeli with red hair, an M-16, and the demeanor of an assassin, approached our car. Nasser rolled down the window, and the man asked for our identification. His finger tapped the trigger. Nasser handed over his Israeli papers identifying him as a Palestinian, and the man took one glance at them and immediately tossed them back into Nasser's lap. "Go!" he said, and gestured his rifle toward the road we had driven in on. "But I have an American," Nasser said. The man had already begun walking back to his outpost.

Nasser got out of his car and started following, but the man became belligerent, pushing him back with the nozzle of his rifle. "Go," the guard shouted. "Go!"

A small van of Israeli settlers approached, and I got out and explained my desire to visit the tomb. The driver offered to give me a ride into town, and Nasser agreed to wait. I climbed into the back of the van along with several students and an old lady. The yellow gate finally slid open.

Kiryat Arba was stunningly beautiful, built on the side of a hill, overlooking a vista of vineyards and orchards that if you squinted looked like Tuscany with all the grass burned off in a fire. The streets were tidy, with gardenias, birds-of-paradise, and bougainvilleas growing in every median and brand-new buildings of freshly hewn limestone on every corner. An old man strolled by accompanied by a small brown dog with a curlicue tail. Two women pushed prams. It all looked so quaint, as long as you didn't notice the barbed wire and three layers of fences.

The driver parked and took me inside a police bureau, where a handful of men tried to decide what to do with me. They huddled, flipped open their mobiles, and talked in hushed tones. Finally they decided I should go stand beside the bank and wait for a bus or a tram to take me down the hill to the Tomb of the Patriarchs. "You won't have to wait for more than ten minutes," they said. "But how will I know what's a tram, what's a bus?" I said. "Don't worry," they said. "There are only Jewish people here." Again, their words were intended as comfort.

Down by the bank, a handful of women were waiting on the corner. I asked if I was in the right place. They didn't answer. A station wagon approached, the women flagged it down like a taxi, then stepped inside. Was this the tram? I wondered. The bus? It didn't matter, there was no room for me anyway.

As the car departed I heard some leaves rustling on the sidewalk. I look around and noticed the streets were empty. There were no cars, no people, no cute little dogs. Kiryat Arba was suddenly quiet, and I realized I was in the one situation I had most wanted to avoid.

I was alone.

My first reaction was fear. A war zone is like a desert, it occurred to me, you can never survive by yourself. But just as quickly the fear receded and was replaced with a cool sensation of calm, like the feeling of my mother's hand on the back of my neck when I was a sick boy. Maybe the feeling came from what the men had said: I was still in Jewish territory. Maybe it came from what Nasser had said: We have no control over our money, our marriage, our death.

Or maybe it came from spending so much time around Abraham, finding comfort in being alone, in breaking away. I thought back to my Bar Mitzvah. Is this what my father had in mind when he urged me to "Go forth"? Probably not. And yet here I was, feeling protected by him, and by that very act.

A few minutes later a rickety Toyota pickup truck approached. I stuck out my hand as I had seen the women do. The driver beckoned me inside. He was an older man, with a knit **kippah** and a long, gray beard. He looked like a piece of driftwood. He had no radio, no air-conditioning, his truck was covered in dust. He proceeded down the disputed hill, with bombed-out buildings and sentry posts every few hundred yards. I looked, and looked, but I didn't know what I was looking for. I heard a gunshot far away. A band of Palestinian teenagers stared angrily as we passed.

Finally we reached the bottom of the hill and the large flagstone plaza at the entrance to the tomb that on festival days can hold up to ten thousand people. I thanked the man and stepped out of the car. WELCOME TO HEBRON, the sign said. The plaza was empty.

On the last Sunday in March 2000, Pope John Paul II shuffled down the plaza of the Western Wall, reached out a trembling hand to touch its stones, and, as is the custom of Jewish visitors, tucked a note to God into a crevice. The pope's pilgrimage, the first ever by a pontiff to the Jewish state, was celebrated with days of interfaith prayer, delicately worded diplomatic niceties, and, inevitably, a tad of squabbling. The visit is seen by many as the highest point yet in the history of dialogue among the monotheistic religions. His written prayer, which was later removed and placed in Yad Vashem, Jerusalem's Holocaust museum, is the clearest manifesto the movement has ever had.

> **God of our fathers, you chose Abraham and his descendants to bring your name to the nations. We are deeply saddened by the behavior of those who in the course of history have caused these children of yours to suffer. And asking your forgiveness, we wish to commit ourselves to genuine brotherhood with the people of the covenant.**

The ideal that the monotheistic religions could live alongside one another without compromising their beliefs and without killing one another shows faint traces in history. It was discussed by Cardinal Nicholas of Cusa in the fifteenth century and touched upon in the Council of Trent in the sixteenth century. But true ecumenical understanding did not begin in earnest until the late nineteenth century.

The word **ecumene,** from French meaning "the whole inhabited earth," was initially used in the Middle Ages to mean **universal** and was later adopted by the Catholic Church to signify its claim to represent the entire world. The word was appropriated by Protestants in the late 1800s to signal their desire to unify the Christian world once again. **Ecumenical** now meant "above and beyond denomination," and ultimately came to mean "above and beyond any particular religion."

In 1893, as part of the world's fair in Chicago to mark the four hundredth anniversary of Columbus's voyage to America, a lawyer named Charles Bonney proposed inviting members of all major religions to the event. The Parliament of the World's Religions is widely regarded as the beginning of the interfaith movement. It was followed by the first World Missionary Conference in Edinburgh (1910), the first World Congress of Faiths (1933), and, after the religious persecution of World War II, the first World Council of Churches in Geneva (1948).

For the most part, the force behind these early meetings was Protestants who aimed to bring together disparate factions of Christianity into a unified mission of action and confession. As a bonus, they hoped to unite Christians with believers of other faiths—including Buddhists, Hindus, and others—into what the World Congress of 1933 called, in an alarming portent of the often lifeless language that would dog this movement, a "spiritual Oneness of the Good Life Universal."

The Catholic Church at first dismissed the movement as "pan-Christians" producing a false understanding of God. But the Holocaust, coupled with the growing influence of prosperous and more pluralistic American Catholics, forced change. At the Second Vatican Council in 1962, the Church would issue its own "Decree of Ecumenism" to restore unity among Christians. The new doctrine also praised Jews as "the people most dear" to God because they received his covenant first. It hailed Muslims as those who "profess to hold the faith of Abraham and together with us adore the one, merciful God."

Vatican II accelerated not just a dialogue among religions but a wholesale reexamination of theology that set out to expunge the angry exclusivism of the past. As the great Christian theologian Walter Brueggemann, of Georgia's Columbia Theological Seminary, said to me when I asked him about the problem of competing traditions, and specifically competing Abrahams: "It is perfectly legitimate for Christians—and I say this as a confessing Christian—to draw all of these traditions to Jesus. It is perfectly legitimate for Jews to draw these traditions toward them, and the same for Muslims. It is not legitimate for Christians or anyone else to presume that theirs is the only direction. The mistake that hegemonic Christianity has made is to act as though our twisting of the tradition is the only way the traditions can be twisted."

The key, Brueggemann said, is to recognize that each religion is an interpretive venture. "I don't have to kill for it, and I don't have to die for it, and I can pay attention to how somebody else did it and entertain that they had reasons for doing what they did as well. I have to be bilingual enough to notice that our confiscation of the tradition is not the only possible legitimate confiscation of the tradition."

Not everyone has welcomed these goals, of course. Some Jews have worried that the interfaith movement—like interfaith marriage and assimilation in general—is just another route to undermine their outnumbered faith. Some Christians have worried that recognition of truth in other religions might undermine the unique relationship between God and Jesus. Some Muslims have worried that identifying too closely with the followers of earlier prophets might dishonor the preeminence of Muhammad.

Altogether, Brueggemann and others speculate, the percentage of believers who would agree to the principle of spiritual parity among the faiths probably totals around two-thirds of Jews, half of Christians, and a third of Muslims. As the Reverend Dr. Wood pointed out, triumphalism has yet to be extinguished entirely; "it's more pronounced in Islam today than in Christianity, and it's more pronounced in Christianity than in Judaism." Rabbi Rosen was even bleaker, citing the reluctance of the Muslim world to embrace liberal democracy in general. "I'm afraid Islam is a couple of hundred years behind us," he said.

As Sheikh Abdul Rauf, a native Kuwaiti who now heads a mosque in New York, observed, most Muslims have yet to experience the economic opportunity or sufficient education to be able to understand, much less implement, the ideals of pluralism and coexistence. "In the same way that American Catholics shaped Vatican II," he said, "and American Jews influence world Judaism with modern ideas like the Reform movement, American Muslims must redefine Islam to include separation of church and state, as well as human rights. The future of Islam lies in the West, in a prosperous community of believing Muslims who have a strong, open-minded voice."

Because of these disparities among believers, as well as the sheer legacy of hostility, advocates of interreligious dialogue have struggled to find a common language. Some have tried to gloss over variances and produce manifestos of shared ideals. This effort often yields bland paeans to loving one's neighbor, not murdering people, and striving toward the "spiritual Oneness of the Good Life Universal." As Harvard's Jon Levenson told me, 90 percent of interfaith dialogue is bunk.

What Levenson, and almost everyone else I talked to about this process, advocated was a different kind of conversation, one that did not minimize differences but accentuated them. One that did not ignore the variations among the routes to God but stressed that even the **idea** of other routes is acceptable. "We should indeed keep the differences there," Rabbi Rosen said, "and learn to respect them. Each religion has its **particular** approach to God. But we also have a **universal** dimension to our traditions that we share, and we must emphasize that as well. That, I would say, is the charge of the hour."

And to fulfill that charge, the leaders of the interfaith conversation realized they needed more than just mandates and dictums. They needed a common source. They needed a foundation that all three traditions revered equally, that embodied the monotheistic ideals of faith in God and righteous behavior toward humanity, and that existed **before** the religions themselves existed.

They needed Abraham.

I started up the stairs toward the entrance to the tomb, an imposing building that looks like a cross between a fortress and a castle. Built by Herod, who also expanded the Second Temple, the three-story structure has casing stones the size of refrigerators, two towers on either end, and storybook crenellations around the top of the entire perimeter. A lone worshiper in a dark coat stood along the base of the wall, while a donkey strolled behind him.

At the entrance, about a dozen Israeli soldiers stood behind a bank of four unused metal detectors. They informed me I would not be allowed to take my knapsack into the shrine and must leave it at the visitors' center back on the road where the truck dropped me off. But it was too dangerous to walk back by myself, they suggested, so four armed men—four—with rifles and combat helmets escorted me down the stairs I had just walked up, waited for me to leave my bag, then chaperoned me back to the entrance. "Pretty quiet day," I said, hopefully.

"Keep walking," the commander said.

After three more layers of security, a body check, and a short interview, I finally stepped inside the door. The Tomb of the Patriarchs and Matriarchs is called El-Haram el-Ibrahami in Arabic, meaning the Sanctuary or Mosque of Abraham; in Hebrew it's called the Machpelah, a word implying **doubling,** for the couples buried here. The site is a three-dimensional model of the history of interfaith relations. Jews built the original shrine; Byzantine Christians rebuilt it as a church; medieval Muslims rebuilt it as a mosque.

Though Muslims kept Jews out during their reign, they did let Jews pray along the exterior, a rare allowance. When Jews reclaimed the site in 1967, they actually allowed the Muslim religious trust to retain majority control of the building against the wishes of right-wing Israelis. For nearly three decades Muslims and Jews prayed alongside each other, the only site in the world where this happened. After Dr. Baruch Goldstein, a radical Jewish settler, massacred twenty-nine Muslims inside the tomb in 1994, the building was divided. One half is controlled by Muslims, the other by Jews. Each community has unrestricted access to the entire facility for roughly a dozen days a year. This gerrymandered solution, though it pleases no one entirely, actually makes the tomb a working model of coexistence—messy, but functioning.

In a way, Hebron has always represented the ache for lost perfection. Jewish tradition says that the Machpelah is located over the entrance to the Garden of Eden. One day Abraham was searching for a missing lamb and came upon a cave. Inside he saw a ray of light and smelled the most beautiful fragrance. Following the light, he met Adam and Eve and knew he wanted to be buried here. After all the divisiveness in his life, Abraham longs to return to the earliest, most unified spot on earth, Paradise.

On this morning Paradise was far away. The only fragrance was loss. The hive of prayer rooms and stone corridors, normally bustling with minions, was vacant. I walked through the open courtyard on the Jewish side and down two steps into the small room between monuments to Abraham and Sarah. The burial caves themselves are hidden underneath the floor, off-limits. The shrine to Abraham is about the size of a small mausoleum and was covered in dark green cloth and locked away behind brass gates that seemed crusted into place. Arabic script lined the trim near the ceiling.

The room between Abraham's tomb and

Sarah's had been turned into a ramshackle synagogue, with a portable, somewhat beat-up ark, a stack of prayer books, a plastic time chart, and an ornate chair for circumcisions. The walls were painted pea green and orange, and a chandelier that seemed out of some Dickensian parlor dropped down from the ceiling. Half the bulbs were out. With the dust, the emptiness, the few overturned chairs, the room felt like a flea market.

I picked up one of the Bibles and turned to Genesis 23. Immediately after the binding of Isaac, Sarah dies at age one hundred twenty-seven, "in Kiriath-arba—now Hebron." Abraham mourns her, then speaks to the Hittites who live in the area, saying, "I am a resident alien among you; sell me a burial site among you." They reply, "You are the elect of God among us. Bury your dead in the choicest of our burial places." But Abraham turns down the gift and insists on buying a cave, the first and only time he legally possesses the land promised his descendants. He then buries his wife.

Abraham's role as a sort of über-father to the region is subtly apparent in these last biblical passages about his life. He buys Sarah's burial cave (where he will ultimately be buried as well) from the Hittites, a Mesopotamian people who must have migrated to Canaan as he had. He and his family will rest forever on surrogate Mesopotamian soil; they will always be strangers in the Promised Land. Moreover, after burying Sarah, he goes on to marry a woman named Keturah, and has six more children. The name Keturah appears to derive from the word **ketoret,** or incense, and seems to link Abraham even more deeply with Arabia because their children have names associated with other Arabian places, such as Midian and Sheba.

Finally, in Genesis 25, verse 7, Abraham dies at one hundred seventy-five years old. The fact that he's far younger than Adam (nine hundred and thirty years), Noah (nine hundred and fifty years), and even his father (two hundred and five years) suggests Abraham is moving from the realm of mythical ideal to a more recognizably human figure. Moreover, after all the dramas in his life, he dies "at a good ripe age, old and contented." He dies at peace.

Even better, his death promotes peace. At Abraham's burial, his two most prominent sons, rivals since before they were born, estranged since childhood, scions of rival nations, come together for the first time since they were rent apart nearly three-quarters of a century earlier. The text reports their union without comment. "His sons Isaac and Ishmael buried him in the cave of

Machpelah, in the field of Ephron son of Zohar the Hittite, facing Mamre, in the field that Abraham had bought from the Hittites."

But the meaning of this moment cannot be diminished. Abraham achieves in death what he could never achieve in life: a moment of reconciliation between his two sons, a peaceful, communal, side-by-side flicker of possibility in which they are not rivals, scions, warriors, adversaries, children, Jews, Christians, or Muslims. They are brothers. They are mourners.

In a sense they are us, forever weeping for the loss of our common father, shuffling through our bitter memories, reclaiming our childlike expectations, smiling, laughing, sobbing, furious and full of dreams, wondering about our orphaned future, and demanding the answers we all crave to hear: What did you want from me, Father? What did you leave me with, Father?

And what do I do now?

The cry of Abraham's children at the death of their father is the cry of their father before they were born: "Help!"

As I was reading a man came into the small sanctuary. Middle-aged, he was wearing a light blue dress shirt, a pair of baggy navy blue trousers, and a **kippah** over his graying, slightly disheveled hair. He rolled up his sleeve and wrapped **teffilin,** leather prayer boxes, around his left arm. He pushed his **kippah** back and strapped a similar box to his forehead. Then he pulled out a small book and proceeded to recite a prayer, bowing several times as he did, oblivious to me, murmuring and occasionally moaning a particular line.

"I can't say I feel close to Abraham every time I pray," Daniel Ginsburg said when he finished. Ginsburg, an American, was a settler in the tinderbox Jewish settlement of a few hundred people in the heart of disputed Hebron itself, just steps from the tomb. "But sometimes I do. We circumcised my youngest son in this room, and it was special."

I asked how he was coping with the situation. "Are you afraid?" I asked.

"It's not a question of afraid," he said, his voice jaded like that of a New York deli attendant. "If you're afraid it's very difficult to live here at all. More concerned, yes. More aware, yes. Taking more precautions, yes. But I don't think that translates into raw fear. If they're shooting outside, you don't go out and say, 'Here I am!'

"My apartment has sandbags in it," he continued, "because ninety-nine percent of my windows face the hills where they shoot at us from. So we have no light. When I first brought in the sandbags, I was told it was enough to put them up to regular height. So I left a little hole so we could have some light in the room, and one of the terrorists found the hole and pumped a few bullets through it and almost killed two of my kids."

He asked why I had traveled to Hebron in the middle of the war, and we began discussing Abraham. At one point we opened the text to the moment when Isaac and Ishmael bury their father. "Is that a hopeful moment?" I asked.

"If you're asking, Can Jews and Muslims live together," he said, "we have. Jews and Muslims lived together in Hebron for hundreds of years before there was a State of Israel. The only way to live in this land is to be open enough to live together."

"So can there be discussion among the faiths?"

"Of course there can be. On a personal level, two people of any faith, or any political persuasion, can sit down, have civil conversation, and even reach civil conclusions. But moving it to a national sphere . . . ? Never happen. First of all, there's always a question about the sincerity of the people involved. I don't know what's in his heart. If you look back at our relations, they've never given me a reason to believe. So can there be a dialogue? Sure, but give me a receipt. Say something to obligate yourself. Then uphold your obligation for a little while. The Arabs have never done it. Study the whole history of Islam and they've never done it."

I felt that familiar heaviness grip our conversation, the same one I had felt a few days earlier with the imam in East Jerusalem, the same one I had experienced many times, over so many years in the region. It was the feeling of interchange giving way to polemic. But this time I also felt something different. I felt that I didn't have to succumb. I felt buttressed by my own experience, by my own newfound knowledge that each religion had a similar strand of chauvinism. And I felt confident in my growing conviction that such rigidity need not be the only path.

"So do you think Abraham is a good vessel for conversation?" I asked.

"If you want to try to figure out from the biblical story if we can live together, I think it's clear that the Bible shows us the personalities of the two peoples. There's an old saying: 'What happened to the forefathers will happen to the sons.' A lot of it bears true. The Muslims are very aggressive, like Ishmael, and they have swords raised against everyone. And the Jews are very passive, like Isaac, who nearly allows himself to be killed without talking back. That's why they are killing us, because we don't fight back."

I started to ask another question, but refrained. He sighed, finished stuffing his **teffilin** into a bag, bid me good-bye, and walked out of the room. Alone again, I wasn't agitated or afraid. I wasn't even sad somehow. I had reached a place where I stood contented alongside Abraham's tomb. I did not need to bow to dogmatism, fanaticism, exclusivism, passivism. I did not need to defer to men of hate, men of despair, radical settlers, genocidal imams. I could pray as myself, with my own contradictions, my own creed, my own sense of unease, my own needful dreams. Abraham was my father, too.

Hearing a noise, I looked out into the courtyard. Two students in black suits and white shirts clasped each other's arms and danced in a circle, chanting joyously. For the first time all morning, music filled the air. The funereal mood turned hopeful. As I was watching, a white pigeon with gray speckles around its neck flew into the chamber where I sat. He sailed into the wall, fluttered, crashed into the brass gate, panicked, then soared to the top of the room, flapping his wings faster and faster, spinning in a circle like the boys outside, seeming to twist the room into a vortex as he sucked the air up toward his wings, swirling around in a never-ending cycle, and searching, clamoring, grasping, clawing for what he knew was there: a way out.

After Daniel Ginsburg left, I walked around the tomb for a few minutes, sat with some old men who were praying, and then departed. The soldiers were still sitting by the gate, smoking. Ginsburg was with them, and he offered to give me a lift up to Kiryat Arba. We didn't speak on the way. He drove up through the Disneyfied town and through the yellow gate to Nasser, who was waiting in his car, drinking a generic cola. We started back to Jerusalem. Nasser and I also didn't talk on the way. I didn't look around this time, didn't count the bullet holes or stare at the darkened glass of the cars that passed us. I just looked straight ahead. This time I wanted to be alone.

On the morning of September 11, I watched from the sixteenth floor of my apartment building as the second World Trade Tower collapsed to the ground, kicking up embers and dust like cinders in a fireplace. I stood speechless, not even able to cry, in the apartment of neighbors I had never met. That afternoon I walked along the Hudson River, past a triage center that was empty because bodies never arrived. Thousands of people had come for the same vigil, some in couples, some with babies in strollers. The sky was burnt orange, the air clear. This was before the smoke and smell turned uptown and choked us, a stir of putrid air and sirens.

Like many, I was mute for days, as stories of death and near death among friends spread quickly through the telephones, the smiling photographs of lost loved ones began to appear on light poles around the city, and candles lined the streets. And still the smell lingered.

In time, the feeling that began to rise inside me was one of being trespassed against, of being violated. A physical sensation of being invaded, and afraid. Then one day I recognized that emotion. It's the feeling one has every day in the Middle East—the sense of terror, pride, and connection to a place. September 11, 2001, was the day the Middle East came to America. The tiny, fertile crescent of land that gave birth to the world's great monotheistic religions and, through them, to Western civilization, had now conquered the far side of the earth, a land long blessedly removed from its tensions.

Like the Middle East, America was forged out of the mixture of politics, religion, and geography. The Founding Fathers echoed biblical language by speaking of the United States as having a "covenant with God" and declaring that America would become a "New Promised Land." America would be its own Rock. For most of our history, Americans believed that being a Promised Land meant we stood **apart** from the rest of the world. Now we know otherwise. Middle Eastern sprawl has reached the United States.

The number one question Americans asked after the attack was, Why do they **hate** us so much? People seemed confused by the irrationality of the act. Sure enough, the number one reality one confronts every day in the Middle East is irrationality. Hatred is a daily emotion, fanaticism an hourly occurrence.

Yet this irrationality comes with an unexpected gift. The Middle East is the cradle of God. When life is not defined by reason, money, or box-office receipts, it must be defined by something nonrational. That something is spirit. In America after September 11, people retreated to emotional havens: flag, family, faith. Grown men cried on national television. There was a sudden glorification of irrationality, of raw emotion, of not being able to explain things.

It became commonplace to say that this response was classically **American.** While that may be true, the deepest aspect of that Americanism is our emotionalism, our tribalism, our conviction of being called to a higher purpose, and, above all, our feeling of an intimate connection between our land and God. Only when we understand that about ourselves can we truly understand what we face in our adversaries around the world.

And that, I finally realized, is why I had come on this journey. I had come because I needed to understand the depth of mistrust among the monotheistic religions, and I needed to understand how it was connected to the basic building blocks of my own identity—geography, family, faith. I had come because I felt hatred myself, and because I needed to know if the roots of that feeling also held possibilities for accord. I had come because I wanted to be alone, because at every turning point in my life, only by breaking away from my surroundings could I come to understand myself—and my dilemma—better.

Above all, I came because I needed an anchor. I needed to believe that loving God, that being prepared to sacrifice for that belief, and that believing in peace had not somehow become incompatible. I needed to know that feeling uneasy yet full of hope went back to our earliest selves.

I needed Abraham.

And I found him—not in the books, in the religious leaders, in the caves. Not in any particular place at all. I found him everywhere, in a sense. When I first set out on this journey, I believed Abraham existed in some mysterious place. The Great Abrahamic Hope was out there, an oasis somewhere in the deepest deserts of antiquity, and all we had to do was track him down, unveil him to the world, and his descendants would live in perpetual harmony, dancing "Kumbaya" around the campfire.

That oasis, I realized, is just a mirage.

But Abraham isn't. Abraham **is** like water, I came to believe, but not the oasis I had originally thought. He's a vast, underground aquifer that stretches from Mesopotamia to the Nile, from Jerusalem to Mecca, from Kandahar to Kansas City. He's an ever-present, ever-flowing stream that represents the basic desire all people have to form a union with God. He's a physical manifestation of the fundamental yearning to be descended from a sacred source. He's a personification of the biological need we all share to feel protected by someone, something. Anything.

This perpetual stream of Abrahamic ideals has existed **just under the surface** of the world for as long as humans have told themselves stories. And every generation—at moments of joy and crisis—tapped into the same source. Each generation **chose** an Abraham for itself.

And we can, too. We can tap into the same underground stream and draw out a figure for our times. We can summon our own savior from the sands, and in so doing bring ourselves closer to God. We can, like Abraham, leave behind our native places—our comfortable, even doctrinaire traditions—and set out for an unknown location, whose dimensions may be known only to God but whose mandate is to be a place where God's blessing is promised to all.

In short, we can create Abraham Number Two Hundred Forty-one.

And we must.

So what should our Abraham look like? For starters, he should look like us. He should be a creature of the modern world, informed by our number-crunching mentality—the number of people killed, the number of people under occupation, 1948, 1967, 56.6 K, 9-11. He should be a student of our time, knowing like a savvy, modern-day Zelig that a lot of other people bearing his name are running around the world wreaking havoc in his honor.

But most of all he should embody the timeless values he's represented for four millennia. The Abraham I crave is God-fearing but also God-not-fearing. This Abraham is a wanderer, a man of the frontier, who's prepared to leave the comfort of his family for the sake of the family he wants to create, and who admits that he can't do this alone but needs a partnership with God in order to realize himself more fully. And this Abraham, having given his life over to God, is then prepared to challenge God, in order that God might more fully realize **himself** and renew his commitment to protect humankind.

The Abraham I long for would be a bridge between humanity and the divine, who demonstrates the example of what it means to be faithful but who also delivers to us God's blessing on earth. And this Abraham conveys God's grace through his children, through Ishmael, through Isaac, and who then has so much hallowedness left over that he doles some out to all the members of his household, and then to the children of his second wife. And this Abraham is perceptive enough to know that his children will not always embrace the fullness of God's blessing, they will not endlessly dance "Kumbaya" around the campfire, they will fight, murder, fly planes into buildings, send bombs into schools, and generally try to squander God's generosity.

But this Abraham believes—against all belief—that his children still crave God. They still need the comfort of something greater than themselves, still hold on to some gleam of humanity, still dream of a moment when they stand alongside one another and pray for their lost father and for the legacy of peace among the nations that was his initial mandate from heaven.

This Abraham is not Jew, Christian, or Muslim. He is not flawless; he's not a saint. But he is himself, the best vessel we've got, the father of all.

This Abraham won't be the only Abraham. He won't be the last Abraham. But he is an Abraham for today.

I choose him.

BLESSINGS

I WOULD LIKE TO THANK THE DOZENS OF people who appear by name in this book for taking time out of their lives to discuss these often sensitive topics with openness, honesty, and candor. Avner Goren helped design this journey and nursed many of its ideas to fruition. For help in the Middle East, I am also grateful to Asnat Cohen, Smadar Goren, Yossi Klein Halevi, Edith Sabbagh, Rabbi Barnea Selavan, and Jonathan Steinberg. In the United States, I received advice and guidance from the Reverend Thomas Breidenthal, Rabbi Abraham Cohen, Adela Collins, John Esposito, Robert Franklin, Melvin Meyer, Robin and Shimon Neustein, Sarah Bowen Savant, and Elsie Stern.

David Black is my friend, counselor, and professional partner. We are joined by the remarkable team of Leigh Ann Eliseo, Gary Morris, Susan Raihofer, Jason Sacher, and Joy Tutela.

Trish Grader committed deeply to this project and helped shape its intellectual and emotional course. Jane Friedman, Cathy Hemming, and Michael Morrison have been steadfast in their support and unwavering in their commitment. Lisa Gallagher and many talented people at HarperCollins/William Morrow have worked tirelessly on my behalf and given me the home I long craved. Debbie Stier and Sharyn Rosenblum, along with DeeDee DeBartlo, Tara Brown, and Claire Greenspan are dedicated and delightful professionals. Special thanks to Betty Lew, Sarah Durand, and Angela Tedesco.

Beth Middleworth is a marvel as a designer and a person.

For their indulgence and camaraderie, thanks to Ruth Reichl, Doc Willoughby, and especially Jane Lear, whose sensitivity and knowledge improved this manuscript tremendously.

Karen Lehrman graciously pushes me to higher standards. Ben Sherwood kindly allows me to travel alongside him on similar paths. For making our work as enjoyable as it is demanding, I am inspired by Karen Essex, David Shenk, and Joe Weisberg. Everlasting thanks also to Laura Benjamin, Susan Chumsky, Suzy Landa, Dana Sade, Lauren Schneider, Jeff Shumlin, Devon Spurgeon, Teresa Tritch, Jane von Mehren, and Bob Wunsch.

Only Linda Rottenberg will ever know the emotional, deeply learned, and profoundly personal wisdom she contributed to this experience. Thank you.

My family continues to indulge, support, and demand more of me—simultaneously. I travel on their shoulders and with their hearts in mine. Special tribute to my brother for personally keeping the red-pen business afloat.

For nearly twenty years I have been blessed with two friends of unrivaled intelligence and uncommon generosity. I met Jessica Korn and Max Stier in the same week, in the same place, exactly half my life ago, and nary a journey—and barely a week—has gone by since when I have not been ennobled by their humanity and goodwill. This book is dedicated to them.

READINGS

ABRAHAM IS SURELY ONE OF THE MOST WRITten about figures in history. I have tried to read widely in the vast literature compiled about him over the centuries. What follows is not a comprehensive bibliography, but a subjective, annotated list of sources I consulted, with special emphasis on ones I relied on most heavily.

First, a few notes. In keeping with longstanding academic custom and recent trends in popular writing, I have used the nonsectarian terms B.C.E. (Before the Common Era) and C.E. (Common Era) in lieu of the terms B.C. and A.D.

For the sake of consistency, all quotations from Genesis and the first five books of the Hebrew Bible come from **The Torah: A Modern Commentary** (New York, 1981), edited by W. Gunther Plaut. Quotations from the rest of the

Hebrew Bible come from **Tanakh: The Holy Scriptures,** the New JPS Translation (Philadelphia, 1985). Quotations from the New Testament come from **The Holy Bible,** the New Revised Standard Version, published by Oxford University Press (New York, 1989). Citations from the Koran come from the Penguin Books version, revised translation by N. J. Dawood (London, 1997).

The reference guides I consulted include the six-volume **Anchor Bible Dictionary**, as well as **The Oxford Companion to the Bible, The Cambridge Companion to the Bible**, and the **Lutterworth Dictionary of the Bible**.

ROCK OF ABRAHAM

I have drawn widely from several popular histories of Abraham, in particular **Abraham** by Karl-Josef Kuschel and **Abraham on Trial** by Carol Delaney. I was also aided by the anthologies **Essays on the Patriarchal Narratives**, edited by A. R. Millard and D. J. Wiseman; **Abrahamic Faiths**, edited by Paul Peachey, George McLean, and John Kromkowski; and **Abraham and Family**, edited by Herschel Shanks.

The Rock by Kanan Makiya is a magical novel that compiles many legends about the Haram al-Sharif. Mircea Eliade's **The Sacred and the Pro-**

fane and **Myth and Reality** are fascinating studies of the symbols of religion.

GOD OF ABRAHAM

Commentaries about Abraham's early life are gathered in the splendid book **The Bible as It Was** by James Kugel and **The Legends of the Jews** by Louis Ginzberg. I continue to draw on the interpretative masterpieces **God** by Jack Miles and **Genesis** by Avivah Zornberg. I also enjoyed **The First Father,** Henry Hanoch Abramovitch's psychological study of Abraham.

There are many helpful studies of Islam, including ones by Karen Armstrong, John Esposito, John Kaltner, and the incomparable Huston Smith, whose **The World's Religions** is an indispensable guide.

CHILDREN OF ABRAHAM

The relationship between Isaac and Ishmael is explored masterfully in **Texts of Terror** by Phyllis Trible. I also consulted **Women's Bible Commentary**, edited by Carol Newsom and Sharon Ringe.

There are any number of examinations of the binding and its relationship to the different religions, including **The Akedah** by Louis Berman and **The Binding and Its Transformation in Judaism and Islam** by Mishal Maswari Caspi and

Sascha Benjamin Cohen. Shalom Spiegel's pioneering study of the Jewish tradition that Abraham may have killed Isaac is **The Last Trial**. Reuven Firestone's monumental work comparing Jewish and Islamic interpretive traditions is **Journeys in Holy Lands**.

For a close reading of the entire Abraham story and a singularly brilliant analysis of the relationship of Abraham to early Judaism and Christianity, I highly recommend Jon Levenson's **The Death and Resurrection of the Beloved Son**.

PEOPLE OF ABRAHAM

Helpful examinations of early Judaism include **A History of Israel** by John Bright and **Rebecca's Children** by Alan Segal. I have relied deeply on **Philo's Place in Judaism**, Samuel Sandmel's study of Abraham's role in Jewish literature, as well as his extremely insightful survey **A Jewish Understanding of the New Testament**.

Abraham's role in Christianity is discussed in depth in **The Figure of Abraham in the Epistles of St. Paul** by Roy Harrisville and **Disinheriting the Jews** by Jeffrey Siker. I have also benefited from studies of Paul made by E. P. Sanders, N. T. Wright, and C. K. Barrett.

Abraham's role in Islam is discussed in **The Seed of Abraham** by Raphael Patai as well as

The Hajj and **Children of Abraham** by F. E. Peters. I also referenced Peters's three-volume **Judaism, Christianity, and Islam**. Bernard Lewis has studied the relationship among the religions in many works; I have benefited tremendously from **The Middle East, The Jews of Islam**, and **Semites and Anti-Semites**.

BLOOD OF ABRAHAM

The relations among the religions in more recent decades have been explored by Karen Armstrong in **The Battle for God** and Samuel Huntington in **The Clash of Civilizations**. The interfaith movement is discussed in **A Wider Faith** by Marcus Braybrooke and **One Earth Many Religions** by Paul Knitter, as well as the benchmark study **The Nature of Doctrine** by George Lindbeck. Yossi Klein Halevi has written a delightful, personal account of worshiping among different faiths in Israel, **At the Entrance to the Garden of Eden**.

To continue the conversations begun with this project, more information is available and comments, inquiries, and observations are welcome at www.brucefeiler.com. That Abraham is still being discussed so widely today may be the best evidence of all that the promise of his blessing has enduring relevance—and the indomitable power to inspire.